IN
THEIR
WORDS

Also by G. M. Best

Non-Fiction

Seventeenth-Century Europe: Documents and Debates
Continuity and Change: A History of Kingswood School 1748-1998
Charles Wesley: A Biography
Shared Aims
Transforming Lives
A Tragedy of Errors: the story of Grace Murray
John Cennick: The Forgotten Evangelist
The Cradle of Methodism : A history of the New Room and of
Methodism in Bristol and Kingswood

Historical Guides

John Wesley: a tercentenary commemorative study
Wesley and Kingswood in Methodism and Education:
From Roots to Fulfillment
The Seven Sisters
Susanna Wesley
Charles Wesley

Children's Book

Gospel's Story

Musical

Marley's Ghosts

Novels

Oliver Twist Investigates
Wuthering Heights Revisited
The Jacobite Murders
The Barchester Murders

In Their Words

The Story Of Early Methodism

In 500 readings selected
from the writings of
John and Charles Wesley
and their contemporaries

G.M.BEST

NEW ROOM PUBLICATIONS
BRISTOL

NEW ROOM PUBLICATIONS

In Their Words
First published 2018

New Room Publications is an imprint of Tangent Books
Unit 5.16 Paintworks
Bristol BS4 3EH
0117 972 0645
www.tangentbooks.co.uk
Email: richard@tangentbooks.co.uk

ISBN 9781910089804

Author: Gary Best

Design: Joe Burt (www.wildsparkdesign.com)

Contents

emphasis on perfection – the expulsion of John Cennick and the break with the Calvinistic Methodists

INTRODUCTION

This book presents the beginnings of Methodism in the eighteenth century in the words of those who experienced it – its leaders, its adherents, its observers, and its opponents. The most quoted individual is John Wesley, but I have also drawn very extensively from the writings of Charles Wesley, whose contribution as preacher and hymn writer, was equally essential, and I have given George Whitefield the attention he deserves but often does not receive. The extent of his role may surprise some readers. Historians have tended to focus almost entirely on John Wesley's contribution and that has given many people the wrong impression that Methodism owed everything entirely to him. Within this book you will find extracts from the writings of one hundred and twenty other individuals and my hope is that the reader will thereby gain a much more vivid impression of the Methodist movement and how it changed lives. While most of the chapters are chronological, four are thematic – one conveying the content of the preaching and its impact, one dealing with the social justice issues raised by Methodism, one covering the amazing role played by the lay preachers, and one providing examples of eighteenth-century prayers. Some readers may wonder why I have chosen certain extracts and not others, but inevitably an editor makes a personal selection. I have not provided detailed source notes but I have provided endnotes to indicate where each extract comes from. I hope you will enjoy the overall result and the many illustrations that accompany the selections.

Gary Martin Best
Historical Consultant and former Warden at the New Room, Bristol

1

THE EARLY LIVES
OF JOHN AND
CHARLES WESLEY
UP TO 1735

A Brand plucked from the Burning 1709 by Henry Perle Parker (Methodist Church House)

Their parents and early life in Epworth

John and Charles were the sons of an Anglican clergyman called Samuel Wesley and his wife, Susanna Annesley. The couple were married on 11 November 1688 and not very long afterwards Samuel became the Rector of St Andrew's Church in the village of Epworth in Lincolnshire. He hated the remote and backward nature of his parish and, though he took his role as Rector seriously, he spent as much time as possible away in London trying in vain to obtain a better appointment:

> I should think it a thousand pities that a man of his brightness, and rare endowments of learning and useful knowledge, in relation to the church of God, should be confined to an obscure corner of the country, where his talents are buried.[1]

Susanna Wesley

St Andrew's Church, Epworth as it stands today

Susanna was the unusually well-educated daughter of Dr Samuel Annesley, a highly regarded and very dedicated nonconformist clergyman in London:

Dr Samuel Annesley (print in New Room)

It is serious Christianity that I press as the only way to better every condition: it is Christianity, downright Christianity, that alone can do it: it is not morality without faith, that is but refined heathenism… [nor] faith without morality, that is but downright hypocrisy. It must be a divine faith, wrought by… [the Holy Spirit] where God and man concur in the operation… a holy faith, full of good works.[2]

Dr Samuel Annesley

Such was his role model and her talent and faith that Susanna very successfully took on the role of preacher when her husband was away, although this ran counter to Church rules:

In your absence I cannot but look upon every soul you leave under my care as a talent committed to me under a trust by the great lord of all the families of heaven and earth… It came into my mind, though I am not a man nor a minister of the gospel, and so cannot be employed in such a worthy employment as they were, yet if my heart were sincerely devoted to God, and if I were inspired with a true zeal for his glory and really did desire the salvation of souls, I might do somewhat more than I do…

Last Sunday I believe we had above two hundred and yet many went away for want of room. [3]   *Susanna Wesley*

Susanna had nineteen pregnancies and ten of their children survived: three sons and seven daughters. All the children respected their father but found him rather autocratic:

Oh, sir, you are a good man! but you are seldom kind and rarely just... You are a tyrant to those you love. [4]   *Mary Wesley*

It was Susanna whom the children most deeply loved and she had very set ideas on what made a good parent:

Susanna Wesley by unknown artist
(Methodist Archives)

Never correct your children to satisfy your passions, but... to reclaim them from their errors and to preserve your authority... Be exceedingly careful to let the measure of your correction be proportionate to the fault, make great allowances for the weakness of their reason and immaturity of judgement, but never spare them through foolish fondness when they sin against God. Instruct them in their duty and reason with them... Cherish the first dawnings of sense and reason, and endeavour to instruct their early years with a sense of religion. 'Train up a child in the way he should go, and when he is old he will not depart from it.'[5]   *Susanna Wesley*

She educated all the children when they were young:

> Learning here placed her richer stores in view...
> winged with love, the minutes gaily flew. [6]   *Hetty Wesley*

Her thinking was a major religious influence on both John and Charles:

> Whatever weakens your reason, impairs the tenderness of your conscience, obscures your sense of God, takes off your relish for spiritual things... is sin to you, however innocent it may seem in itself.[7]
> *Susanna Wesley*

> 'Tis not learning these things by rote, nor the saying a few prayers morning and evening, that will bring you to heaven; you must understand what you say, and you must practise what you know.[8]
> *Susanna Wesley*

> In all things endeavour to act upon principle, and do not live like the rest of mankind, who pass through the world like straws upon a river, which are carried which way the stream or wind drives them.[9]
> *Susanna Wesley*

> Some truths... are of so little importance to the salvation of mankind... that they ought not to be contended for, nor ever asserted at the expense of peace and charity. Let, therefore, the general bent of your mind and conversation tend to peace and unity.[10]
> *Susanna Wesley*

John Wesley, the middle son, was born on 17 June 1703:

> I am a spirit come from God and returning to God; just hovering

over the great gulf, till a few moments hence I am no more seen – I drop into an unchangeable eternity! I want to know one thing, the way to heaven – how to land safe on that happy shore.[11] *John Wesley*

Charles Wesley was born prematurely on 18 December 1707 and ill health was to be a problem throughout his life:

I always find strength for the work of the ministry; but when my work is over, my strength, both bodily and spiritual, leaves me. I can pray for others, not for myself. God by me strengthens the weak hands, and confirms the feeble knees; yet am I myself as a man in whom [there] is no strength. I am weary and faint in mind, longing continually to be discharged. [12] *Charles Wesley*

Section showing John in the painting of the 1709 fire by Henry Perle Parker 1840 (Methodist Church House)

In 1709 John (or Jack as the family called him) narrowly escaped death in a fire at the Epworth Rectory. This may have been started deliberately because many of the parishioners hated Samuel Wesley and wanted to drive him out:

The fire broke out about eleven or twelve o'clock at night, we being all in bed; nor did we perceive it till the roof of the corn chamber was burnt through and the fire fell upon your sister Hetty's bed… She waked and immediately run to call your father… He bid us all shift for life, for the roof was falling fast and nothing but the thin wall kept the fire from the staircase. We had no time to take our clothes, but ran all naked. I called to Betty to bring the children out of the nursery. She took up Patty and left Jacky to follow her. But he, going to the door, and seeing all the fire, ran back again... Your father carried sister Emily, Suky and Patty into the garden; then, missing Jacky, he ran back into the house to see if he could save him. He heard him miserably crying out in the nursery and attempted several times to get upstairs, but was beat back by the flame; then he thought him lost and commended his soul to God... The child climbed up to a window and called out to them in the yard; they got up to the casement and pulled him out just as the roof fell into the chamber... and so by God's mercy we all escaped. [13]   *Susanna Wesley*

John Wesley was brought up to believe God had saved him for a special purpose:

Alleged relics from the 1709 fire on display in the Museum at the New Room

Is not he a brand plucked from the burning? ... I do intend to be more particularly careful of the soul of this child, that thou hast so mercifully provided for, than ever I have been, that I may do my endeavour to instil into his mind the principles of thy true religion and virtue. Lord, give me grace to do it sincerely and prudently, bless my attempts with good success.[14]   *Susanna Wesley*

At school in London

In 1714 John won a scholarship to study at Charterhouse School in London. He found it a place where bullying was rife:

> It is the common law of the place that the young should be implicitly obedient to the elder boys, and this obedience resembles more the submission of a slave to his master... A boy is cast in among five or six hundred other boys, and is left to form his own character... and left to their own crude conceptions and ill-formed propensities... These places of education [offer] a system of premature debauchery... They only prevent men from being corrupted by the world by corrupting them before their entry into the world.[15]
>
> *Sydney Smith*

Charterhouse School from an etching by Robert Havell (public domain)

In 1716 Charles won a scholarship to Westminster School in London and lodged with his eldest brother Samuel, who was the school's head usher (i.e. deputy headmaster) and a fine teacher. Of Samuel's subsequent time as Headmaster of Blundell's School it was said:

He was nearly idolised. His diligence and able method of teaching in his school were so evident and successful... that children were sent from all quarters to be placed under his tuition. His memory was dear to all who had the privilege of his acquaintance. [16]

Adam Clarke

Charles found Westminster School to be a rough place where boys often led each other astray, but he opposed the bullying that was prevalent and he eventually became Head Boy:

> What but a miracle of grace
> could keep my soul within
> the mouth of hell...
> where troops of young corrupters tried
> in wickedness to excel,
> lewdness their vile delight, and pride
> their boasted principle.[17]

Charles Wesley

The schoolroom at Westminster School (public domain)

Samuel Wesley junior encouraged his younger brothers to have a strong social conscience and he helped develop Charles' poetic talent:

Samuel Wesley, brother of John and Charles (New Room Archives and Library)

Through him, principally, were his brothers John and Charles maintained... and in all straits of the family, his purse was not only opened but emptied... And all this was done with so much affection and deep sense of duty... and done so secretly... [that] those alone knew his bounty who were its principal objects, and they were not permitted to record it... His brothers always spoke of him with the highest reverence, respect and affection.[18]

Adam Clarke

The creation of 'the Holy Club'

Christ Church College viewed from Pembroke College in History of Oxford 1814 (New Room Archives and Library)

In 1720 John won a scholarship to Christ Church College in Oxford and for a few years he enjoyed university life to an extent he later regretted:

Too much addicting myself to light behaviour at all times, listening too much to idle talk, and reading vain plays and books.[19]

John Wesley

Oxford University had at this time a reputation for not paying much attention to scholarship or religion:

Satirical print of students at Oxford University by William Hogarth c1736 (New Room Archives and Library)

The public professors... [have] these many years given up altogether the pretence of teaching... Their days are filled by a series of uniform employments: the chapel, the hall, the coffee house and the common room, till they retire, weary and self-satisfied, to a long slumber. From the tasks of reading and thinking or writing, they have absolved their consciences.[20]   ***Edward Gibbon***

John Potter, Bishop of Oxford and later Archbishop of Canterbury copy of portrait in Lambeth Palace (public domain)

By 1725 John had finished his first degree and become more seriously religious and, encouraged by his parents, he took the decision to become a clergyman. The Right Reverend John Potter, Bishop of Oxford, ordained him as a deacon in the Church of England:

The Holy Jesus... seems to have taken the conduct of your soul into his own hand.[21]   ***Susanna Wesley***

In 1726 John became a Fellow of Lincoln College in Oxford and Charles won a scholarship to Christ Church College. On his arrival Charles wanted to enjoy himself as much as his brother had done:

The Wesley Room at Lincoln College restored to commemorate his time as a fellow there

If I spoke to him about religion, he would warmly answer, 'What, would you have me a saint all at once?' and would hear no more.[22]

John Wesley

The Epworth Rectory as it is today

In 1727 John returned to live in Epworth so he could act as his father's curate. This soon led him to seek full ordination as a presbyter (or priest) because deacons are not permitted to offer the sacraments, including baptism, marriage and Holy Communion. He was ordained as the Rev. John Wesley in August 1728 by the Bishop of Oxford:

If you desire to be extensively useful, do not spend your time and strength in contending for or against such things as are of a disputable nature; but in… promoting real, essential holiness. [23]

John Potter, Bishop of Oxford

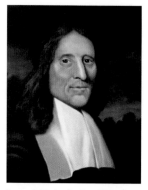

The brothers kept in constant touch and their father recognised just how important their relationship had become for both of them:

I think you'd be either of you like a bird without a wing without the other.[24]

Samuel Wesley

Samuel Wesley by David Keal
2003 (Epworth Rectory)

In 1729 Charles became more serious-minded about his faith and he created a religious society for himself and two of his friends. This was to develop under John's guidance into what other students jokingly called 'the Holy Club' – and the society is now seen as being the precursor of Methodism:

Engraved print of the Holy Club as painted by Marshall Claxton 1858 (Museum at the New Room)

They imagine they cannot be saved if they do not spend every hour, nay minute, of their lives in the service of God. And to that end they read prayers every day in the common gaol, preach every Sunday, and administer the sacrament... They almost starve themselves to be able to relieve the poor and buy books for their conversion. They endeavour to reform notorious whores and allay spirits in haunted houses. They fast two days a week, which has emaciated them to that degree they are a fearful sight... They rise every day at five... and till prayers at eight, they sing psalms and read some pieces of divinity. They met at each other's rooms at six of the clock five nights in the week, and from seven to nine read a piece of some religious book. In short they are so particular that they have become the jest of the whole university.[25]   *Richard Morgan*

The concept of improving one's faith by belonging to a religious society was not new – some clergy, including their father, had long promoted the idea:

I hear my son, John, has the honour of being styled 'the Father of the Holy Club': if it be so, I must be the grandfather of it.[26]
Samuel Wesley

John Gambold in later life (New Room Archives and Library)

Charles' amiable and cheerful character was a key factor in attracting students to join the society:

Charles Wesley was a man made for friendship; who, by his cheerfulness and vivacity, would refresh his friend's heart; with attentive consideration, would enter into and settle all his concerns; so far as he was able, would do anything for him, great or small; and, by a habit of openness and freedom, leave no room for misunderstanding... I never observed a person have a more real deference for another than he constantly had for his brother. Indeed, he followed his brother entirely. Could I describe one of them I should describe both.[27]   *John Gambold*

In 1733 Charles befriended Benjamin Ingham, a student at Queen's College, and George Whitefield, a student at Pembroke College. Both of these were to become leaders within the Holy Club and subsequently vitally important preachers in the eighteenth-century religious revival which created Methodism:

He sent an invitation to me... to come to breakfast with him... .I thankfully embraced the opportunity; and blessed be God! it was one of the most profitable visits I ever made in my life. My soul, at that time, was athirst for some spiritual friends to lift up my hands when they hung down, and to strengthen my feeble knees. He soon discovered it, and, like a wise winner of souls, made all his discourses tend that way... [Being an Oxford Methodist] built me up daily in the knowledge and fear of God... Their hearts glowed with the love of God.' [28]

George Whitefield

The lifestyle of the Oxford Methodists

John recognised that people are creatures of habit and so it made sense for Christians to try and be as methodical as possible in fulfilling their religious duties. He asked the members of his and Charles' religious society to set aside regular times for reading the Bible, praying, and so on. Other students began describing them as 'Methodists', possibly as a jibe against their daily and weekly routines.

It was not a name that either John or Charles welcomed. One of John's tutees found it very difficult to cope with such mocking:

> The whole college makes a jest of me… By becoming his pupil I am stigmatised with the name of a Methodist, the misfortune of which I cannot describe… I think it incumbent upon me to inform you that it is my opinion that if I am continued with Mr Wesley I shall be ruined. [29]
>
> *Richard Morgan*

John Wesley based on portrait by John Williams 1742 (originally part of collection of Wesley College, Bristol)

John's routines – which in the future were to be frequently restated by him and incorporated into many of Charles' hymns – started with regular prayer, both morning and evening:

God does nothing but in answer to prayer, and everything with it. [30]

John Wesley

The ruins of my soul repair and make my heart a house of prayer. [31] *Charles Wesley*

Equally vital was not only reading the Bible daily but also understanding it. This was achieved by meditation, by studying commentaries and other religious books, and by consulting others:

> At any price, give me the book of God!... Let me be 'homo unius libri' [a man of one book]… I sit down alone… [and in God's] presence I open, I read his book… Is there a doubt concerning the meaning of what I read? Does anything appear dark or

intricate?… I then search after and consider parallel passages of Scripture, 'comparing spiritual things with spiritual'. I meditate thereon, with all the attention and earnestness of which my mind is capable. If any doubt remains, I consult those who are experienced in the things of God.[32]   *John Wesley*

> Bid me in the sacred leaves
> trace the way to paradise,
> all his oracles explore,
> read, and pray them o'er and o'er. [33]   *Charles Wesley*

John urged all members to keep a journal so they could record their spiritual progress and he suggested they should daily ask themselves the following 22 questions:

1. Am I consciously or unconsciously creating the impression that I am better than I really am? In other words, am I a hypocrite?
2. Am I honest in all my acts and words, or do I exaggerate?
3. Do I confidentially pass on to others what has been said to me in confidence?
4. Can I be trusted?
5. Am I a slave to dress, friends, work or habits?
6. Am I self-conscious, self-pitying, or self-justifying?
7. Did the Bible live in me today?
8. Do I give the Bible time to speak to me every day?
9. Am I enjoying prayer?
10. When did I last speak to someone else of my faith?
11. Do I pray about the money I spend?
12. Do I get to bed on time and get up on time?
13. Do I disobey God in anything?
14. Do I insist upon doing something about which my conscience

is uneasy?

15. Am I defeated in any part of my life?
16. Am I jealous, impure, critical, irritable, touchy or distrustful?
17. How do I spend my spare time?
18. Am I proud?
19. Do I thank God that I am not as other people, especially as the Pharisees who despised the publican?
20. Is there anyone whom I fear, dislike, disown, criticise, hold a resentment toward or disregard? If so, what am I doing about it?
21. Do I grumble or complain constantly?
22. Is Christ real to me?[34]

John Wesley

Part of the display on the Holy Club and its members in the Museum at the New Room

He urged all to share their faith with others whenever an opportunity arose:

When the occasion offers… speak, though it is pain and grief to you; and it will be[come] easier and easier. [35]
John Wesley

My gracious master and my God assist me to proclaim,
to spread through all the earth abroad the honours of your name.[36]
Charles Wesley

M stands for 'a Methodist parson, stark mad!' in Richard Newton's 1795 'A Clerical Alphabet' (New Room Archives and Library)

The Oxford Methodists met up together at least once or twice a week so they could offer each other support and guidance. This was to become a main feature of the subsequent Methodist movement:

Strengthen you one another. Talk together as often as you can. And pray earnestly with and for one another. [37] *John Wesley*

Help us to help each other, Lord, each other's cross to bear;
let each his friendly aid afford, and feel his brother's care.
Help us to build each other up, our little stock improve;
increase our faith, confirm our hope, and perfect us in love. [38]

Charles Wesley

Charles Wesley as painted by Thomas Hudson 1749 (Museum at the New Room)

Members were expected to go to the University Church of St Mary the Virgin every week and to receive Holy Communion as often as they could (churches at this time did not offer communion very often). Regularly receiving Holy Communion remained a central demand of Methodism:

Oxford Castle as it is today. In the eighteenth century it was a prison, which John and Charles and other Oxford Methodists regularly visited

If we desire the pardon of our sins, if we wish for strength to believe, to love and obey God, then we should neglect no opportunity of receiving the Lord's Supper.[39]
John Wesley

O the depth of love divine, the unfathomable grace!
Who shall say how bread and wine God into us conveys!
How the bread his flesh imparts, how the wine transmits his blood,
fills his faithful people's hearts with all the life of God!...
Sure and real is the grace, the manner be unknown...
Let us taste the heavenly powers, Lord, we ask for nothing more.
Thine to bless, 'tis only ours to wonder and adore.[40]
Charles Wesley

The Oxford Methodists were also expected to fast once or twice per week:

[Some have] exalted this beyond all Scripture and reason, and others [have] utterly disregarded it... as if it were nothing, as if it were a fruitless labour... The truth lies between them both... It is not all, nor yet is it nothing... It is... a precious means... which God himself has ordained, and in which therefore, when it is duly used, God will surely give us his blessing. [41]

John Wesley

University Church of St Mary the Virgin, Oxford as it is today (Tony Hisgett: Creative Commons)

And to constantly engage in helping others, particularly the poor, sick, uneducated, and imprisoned:

See that your heart is filled at all times and on all occasions with real, genuine benevolence.... Let it pant in your heart, let it sparkle in your eyes, let it shine in your actions. [42]

John Wesley

> To serve the present age,
> my calling to fulfill,
> O may it all my powers engage
> to do the Master's will.[43]

Charles Wesley

Almost all of the features of Christian living associated with Methodism were therefore first laid down as rules for those belonging to the Holy Club.

2

THE BEGINNINGS OF
THE METHODIST
MOVEMENT
1735-39

Sections from engravings of Bristol from the north-west and the south-east in an engraving produced in 1734 (Bristol Reference Library)

The American Adventure

On 25 April 1735 Samuel Wesley senior died:

> You have reason to envy us, who could attend him in the last stage of his illness. The few words he could utter I saved, and hope never to forget... He appeared full of faith and peace... [and] often laid his hand upon my head, and said, 'Be steady. The Christian faith will surely revive in this kingdom. You shall see it, though I shall not.' When we were met about him, his usual expression was, 'Now let me hear you talk upon heaven'.[44]
>
> *Charles Wesley*

General James Edward Oglethorpe by Alfred Edmund Dyer (public domain)

The family had to leave Epworth Rectory because John had selfishly refused to take over from his father as Rector, preferring his lifestyle in Oxford. In August John, partly out of remorse, decided that he and Charles should go as missionaries to the newly founded colony of Georgia in North America, where they would work under the direction of its creator, General Oglethorpe:

> My chief motive, to which all the rest are subordinate, is the hope of saving my own soul. I hope to learn the true sense of the Gospel of Christ by preaching it to the heathen. *John Wesley*

At John's insistence Charles agreed to become a clergyman, though he had no desire to take on that role. Prior to their departure he was ordained as a deacon and then as a presbyter by the Right Rev. Edmund Gibson, Bishop of London. Given Charles' frail health, their brother Samuel felt 'Jack' (as John was known within the family) was recklessly risking Charles' life:

> Jack knew his strength and used it… I freely own 'twas the will of Jack, but am not yet convinced 'twas the will of God.[45]
>
> *Samuel Wesley Jr*

The Wesleys and their friends embarking on the 'Symonds' (Wesley His Own Biographer 1893)

On 14 October 1735 John and Charles embarked on the ship the 'Symonds' for Georgia with two of their friends, Benjamin Ingham and Charles Delamotte. On ship they came into regular contact with a small group of German-speaking Moravian missionaries. Many of the religious practices of the Moravians were to have a deep influence on their lives:

> They are more like the primitive Christians than any church now existing… They live together in perfect love and peace, having for the present all things in common. They are more ready to serve their neighbours than themselves. In business they are diligent, in all their dealings strictly just; and in everything they behave themselves with meekness, sweetness and humility.[46]
>
> *Benjamin Ingham*

Count Nicholas von Zinzendorf (New Room Archives and Library)

The Moravians traced their religious roots back to 'the Unitas Fratrum' (the Unity of the Brethren), a very early Protestant movement, but they belonged to an organisation which had been created in 1727 in Saxony by Count Nicholas von Zinzendorf, a Lutheran who was greatly influenced by the German Pietist movement. He was to develop his renewed version of 'the Unitas Fratrum' into a separate 'Moravian Church' in 1741. Zinzendorf's vision was to create communities based on the lifestyle of the first Christians:

There can be no Christianity without community.[47]

Nicholas von Zinzendorf

He was sending out small groups of Moravians to areas where there was no organised church in order to spread the gospel message:

Meeting with the Moravians on board ship (Wesley His Own Biographer 1893)

Remember, you must never use your position to lord it over the heathen. Instead, you must humble yourself and earn their respect through your own quiet faith and the power of the Holy Spirit. The missionary must seek nothing for himself, no seat of honour or hope of fame… You must be content to suffer, to die, and to be forgotten.[48]

Nicholas von Zinzendorf

A huge storm at sea threatened to destroy the ship on 25 January 1736. John and Charles were amazed by the calm shown by the Moravians and were very impressed by the power of hymn-singing to strengthen faith. This was a new experience for them because the Church of England, while content to use hymns as a source of meditation, disapproved of public hymn singing on the grounds that only things written in the Bible (such as the psalms) should be used within a church. This was a common view because the Catholic Church had for centuries banned hymns and the Protestant reformer, Jean Calvin, had upheld that approach. The only Protestants to sing hymns were therefore those who looked for guidance to the sixteenth-century reformer and hymn writer, Martin Luther:

The winds roared round about us, and – what I had never heard before – whistled as distinctly as it had been a human voice. The ship not only rocked to and fro with the utmost violence, but shook and jarred

The storm crossing the Atlantic (New Room Archives and Library)

with so unequal, grating a motion, that one could not but with great difficulty keep one's hold of anything, nor stand a moment without it. Every ten minutes came a shock against the stern or side of the ship, which one would think should dash the planks in a thousand pieces… In the midst of the psalm wherewith their service began… the sea broke over, split the mainsail in pieces, covered the ship, and poured in between the decks as if the great deep had already swallowed us up. A terrible screaming began among the English. The Germans calmly sang on.[49] *John Wesley*

Charles preaching to the native Americans (New Room Archives and Library)

From February to July 1736 John and Charles Delamotte based themselves in Savannah while Charles Wesley and Benjamin Ingham went with General Oglethorpe to a new settlement called Fort Frederica. Charles became the target of the hostility of a small group of colonists and his health collapsed. By the end of July he was forced to leave Georgia and begin the journey back to Britain:

> [I was] abused and slighted… [and] trampled upon… The people have found out that I am in disgrace… My few well-wishers are afraid to speak to me. Some have turned out of the way to avoid me… The servant that used to wash my linen sent it back unwashed.[50]   *Charles Wesley*

En route home Charles stopped off in Charleston and was horrified by what he saw and heard about slavery:

> One Colonel Lynch is universally known to have cut off a poor negro's legs; and to kill several of them every year by his barbarities… Mr. Hill, a dancing-master in Charlestown, whipped a she-slave so long that she fell down at his feet for dead. When by the help of a physician she was so far recovered as to show signs of life, he repeated the whipping with equal rigour, and concluded with dropping hot sealing wax upon her flesh. Her crime was overfilling a tea-cup.[51]   *Charles Wesley*

Isaac Watts portrait by unknown artist (National Portrait Gallery)

In 1737 John produced the first ever American hymnbook – a compilation of 78 hymns printed in Charleston. It contained nothing written by Charles because he had not yet embarked on hymn-writing, but it included eight hymns translated by John from German, Spanish and French sources. The authorities disapproved of its publication because of the Church's opposition to public hymn-singing. Almost half of the hymns John chose to include were ones written thirty years earlier by a nonconformist minister, Issac Watts, the man now known as 'the godfather of English hymnody':

> When I survey the wondrous cross
> on which the Prince of Glory died,
> my richest gain I count but loss,
> and pour contempt on all my pride.
>
> Forbid it, Lord, that I should boast,
> save in the death of Christ my God:
> all the vain things that charm me most,
> I sacrifice them to his blood…
>
> Were the whole realm of Nature mine,
> that were a present far too small;
> love so amazing, so divine,
> demands my soul, my life, my all.[52]

Isaac Watts

In the spring of 1736 John had agreed to tutor Sophy Hopkey, the seventeen year-old niece of the colony's magistrate, and he began to court her, although he had vowed never to marry:

> My desire and design still was to live single… [but] she came to me every morning and evening… I found it a task too hard for me… [because] in such intimacy of conversation as ours was… I could not avoid using some familiarity or other… Sometimes I put my arm around her waist, sometimes took her by the hand, and sometimes kissed her.[53]
> *John Wesley*

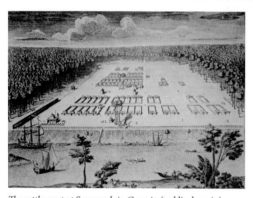

The settlement at Savannah in Georgia (public domain)

His refusal to propose led the colonists to judge that he was playing with her affections and her family insisted on Sophy marrying another man in March 1737. John in his jealousy verbally abused the couple and the colonists put him on trial when the pregnant Sophy had a miscarriage. John was forced to flee back to England. One of the colony's leaders summed up the discontent felt with Wesley:

> I like nothing you do; all your sermons are satires upon particular persons, therefore I will never hear you more; and all the people are of my mind… They cannot tell what religion you are of… They do not know what to make of it… All the quarrels that have been here since your arrival have been because of you… There is neither man nor woman in the town who minds a word

> you say. And so you may preach long enough; but nobody will
> come to hear you.[54]
>
> *William Horton*

Unaware of this, Charles was raising financial support for the colony in London, despite the fact he was still very ill. Out of a mix of loyalty and love, George Whitefield agreed to go out to North America to assist John. This was a surprise to many because Whitefield had been ordained as a deacon and already won a reputation as a great preacher in London and Bristol and he was being offered some very attractive appointments in the Church prior to becoming a presbyter:

George Whitefield by John Wollaston 1742 (National Portrait Gallery)

> Many of all denominations were obliged to return from the churches where I preached for want of room... I was called by the Mayor to preach before him and the Corporation... Large offers were made me, if I would stay in Bristol... All wondered that I would go to Georgia, who might be so well provided for at home! And some urged, if I had a mind to convert Indians, I might go instead among the Kingswood colliers, and find Indians enough. But none of these things moved me.[55]
>
> *George Whitefield*

Charles eventually had to accept that his health would not permit him to return to America and Whitefield set sail without him on 30 December 1737. Just prior to his departure news arrived that John Wesley had unexpectedly returned, but Whitefield felt he could not break the commitment he had made to go. John was devastated at his failure, feeling that all his efforts to please God had come to nothing:

> But what have I learned…? That I, who went to America to convert others, was never myself converted to God… [I] can talk fluently upon spiritual things… I gave all my goods to feed the poor… I have thrown up my friends, reputation, ease, country; I have put my life in my hand, wandering into strange lands; I have given my body to be devoured by the deep, parched up with heat, consumed by toil and weariness… But does all this… make me acceptable to God?… Does all this give me a claim to the holy, heavenly, divine character of a Christian? By no means… My whole heart is 'altogether corrupt and abominable'… [and] I am 'a child of wrath', an heir of hell… If it be said that I have faith… I answer so have the devils… The faith I want is 'a sure trust and confidence in God, that, through the merits of Christ, my sins are forgiven, and I am reconciled to the favour of God'.[56]
>
> *John Wesley*

Hearts Strangely Warmed

Peter Bohler (New Room Archives and Library)

In January 1738 a Moravian called Peter Bohler began trying to convince John and Charles that they were making a big mistake in trying to earn their salvation. He encouraged them to study the writings of Martin Luther on 'justification by faith' (i.e. that a forgiving God offers salvation to all who put their faith in him, despite human sinfulness). In his depression John contemplated ceasing to be a preacher:

> It struck into my mind, 'Leave off preaching. How can you preach to others, who have not faith yourself?... [But Bohler] said 'Preach faith till you have it; and then, because you have it, you will preach faith'.[57]
>
> *John Wesley*

John and Charles formally resigned from their American commitments and joined up with Bohler in creating a religious society in Fetter Lane in London based on Moravian organisation and patterns of worship. They encouraged former Oxford Methodists to join it and the society attracted not only Germans but Huguenots (as French Protestants were called):

> Peter Bohler... amazed me more and more by the account he gave of living faith – the holiness and happiness which he affirmed to attend it. [58]
>
> *John Wesley*

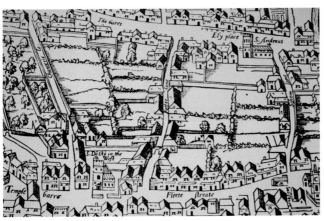

The location of Fetter Lane in London in sixteenth-century Agas map from 1874 print. It runs north-south between Holburn Street and Fleet Street (public domain)

On 21 May 1738 Charles had a deep religious experience in which he realised he did not have to earn his salvation. All he had to do was put his trust in God's love and forgiveness. This was the experience that released all Charles' talents first as a hymn writer and then as a preacher:

> Long my imprisoned spirit lay,
> fast bound in sin and nature's night;
> thine eye diffused a quickening ray;
> I woke, the dungeon flamed with light;
> my chains fell off, my heart was free,
> I rose, went forth, and followed thee.[59]   *Charles Wesley*

On 24 May 1738 John had a similar deep religious experience in which he also accepted that a person is saved through faith and not through what a person does:

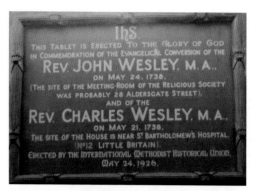

Plaque marking the locations of the life-changing religious experiences of John and Charles

[I have discovered]… the Christian faith is… not only an assent to the whole gospel of Christ, but also a full reliance on the blood of Christ; a trust in the merits of His life, death, and resurrection… [through which a person's] sins are forgiven, and he reconciled to the favour of God.[60]   *John Wesley*

John's experience is still celebrated annually by Methodists on 'Aldersgate Sunday', a name given because of where the event took place:

The Aldersgate Flame outside the Museum of London commemorating Wesley's heart strangely-warmed

In the evening I went very unwillingly to a society in Aldersgate Street, where one was reading Luther's preface to the Epistle to the Romans. About a quarter before nine, while he was describing the change which God works in the heart through faith in Christ, I felt my heart strangely warmed. I felt I did trust in Christ, Christ alone for salvation; and an assurance was given me that He took away my sins, even mine, and saved me from the law of sin and death.'[61]

John Wesley

The first responses of John and Charles to knowing they were saved

Charles' health was still poor so, in June 1738, John went with Benjamin Ingham, who had also returned from America, to visit the Moravian settlements in Germany at Herrnhut and Marienborn and to meet their leader, Count Zinzendorf. They stayed three months. John was further influenced by the Moravians as he witnessed at first hand their organisational effectiveness and their ways of worshipping (e.g. he was impressed by their love feasts, which were an extended communion service based round a simple meal). However, this experience was not enough to convince him to join the Moravian Church when that was subsequently created:

The Moravian settlement at Herrnhut (New Room Archives and Library)

I cannot but rejoice in your steadfast faith, in your love to our blessed Redeemer, your deadness to the world; your meekness, chastity, and love of one another. I greatly approve of your conferences and bands; of your method of instructing children; and in general of your great care of the souls committed to your charge. But… do you not wholly neglect joint fasting? Is not the Count all in all… calling him 'Rabbi'?… Is there not something of levity in your behaviour? Are you, in general, serious enough?… Do you not sometimes fall into trifling conversation? Do you not magnify your own church too much?… Is not the spirit of secrecy the spirit of your community? Have you that childlike openness, frankness, and plainness of speech so manifest to all in the apostles and first Christians?[62]   *John Wesley*

By July Charles was fit enough to commence preaching on 'salvation by faith':

Whether your lives are stained with outward visible enormities, or less observable abominations, it makes no great difference… The careless and the debauched, the scandalous and the reputable sinner, the filthy and the ignorant thoughtless one… turn unto the Lord your God, for he is gracious and merciful, slow to anger and of great kindness… God is not far from every one of you. For you there is about to be joy in heaven, and the angels are tuning their harps… if ye hearken unto God… he can translate thee this moment out of darkness into his marvellous light, out of bondage into the glorious liberty of the sons of God… Pray without ceasing, till he is formed in your hearts by faith.[63]   *Charles Wesley*

He spent much time visiting prisoners in Newgate Prison. The impact on those condemned to die was enormous and Charles accompanied them to their public execution at Tyburn:

> We wrestled in mighty prayer. All the criminals were present,
> and all delightfully cheerful… Joy was visible in all their faces.
> We sang:
>> 'Behold the saviour of mankind,
>> nail'd to the shameful tree!
>> How vast the Love that him inclined
>> to bleed and die for thee! etc'
>
> It was one of the most triumphant hours I have ever known…
> [Afterwards on the scaffold] they were all cheerful; full of
> comfort, peace and triumph; assuredly persuaded Christ had
> died for them and waited to receive them into paradise... None
> showed any natural terror of death – no fear, or crying, or tears…
> I never saw such calm triumph, such incredible indifference to
> dying. We sang several hymns… [and] when the cart drew off,
> not one stirred, or struggled for life, but meekly gave up their
> spirits… That hour, under the gallows was the most blessed
> hour of my life.[64]   ***Charles Wesley***

*The Idle Apprentice executed at Tyburn by William Hogarth in 1747 shows a Methodist
preacher in attendance (Victoria and Albert Museum)*

Edmund Gibson, Bishop of London (public domain)

In September 1738 John arrived back from Germany and he and Charles agreed to regularly attend the Fetter Lane society and to encourage religious societies in London to adopt some features of Moravian organisation and worship, including hymn singing. The church authorities voiced disapproval of their increasing links with 'foreigners'. This disapproval escalated to an even greater level when, in November, Charles preached in the open air to the thousands who had turned up to see a public execution. Although Charles said he would not repeat his action, many clergy began labelling him and John as 'enthusiasts' (i.e. religious fanatics) and refused to let them preach from their pulpits:

> [On 21 October] I waited with my brother on the Bishop of London to answer the complaints he had heard against us... [On 14 November] I had another conference with his Lordship... [He said] 'Don't you know no man can exercise parochial duty in London without my leave?... I have the power to punish'... [I said] 'Does your Lordship charge me with any crime?' [He replied] 'No, no. I charge you with no crime'. [65] *Charles Wesley*

Over Christmas the brothers held celebrations with four of their Oxford friends to mark the temporary return of George Whitefield from America. He had come back so he could be ordained as a presbyter and to raise funds to build an orphanage in the colony of Georgia. On New Years' Eve the friends met up with about sixty Moravians to celebrate the New Year and in the early morning they had a Pentecostal type experience in which they all felt called on by

God to create a religious revival:

> About three in the morning, as we were continuing instant in prayer, the power of God came mightily upon us, insomuch that many cried out for exceeding joy, and many fell to the ground. As soon as we had recovered a little from that awe and amazement at the presence of his majesty, we broke out with one voice, 'We praise thee, O God; we acknowledge thee to be the Lord!'[66]
>
> *John Wesley*

Open-air preaching in Bristol

Martin Benson, Chaplain to the Prince of Wales and Bishop of Gloucester (public domain)

In January 1739 George Whitefield was ordained as a presbyter by Martin Benson, the Bishop of Gloucester:

> I think him a very pious, well-meaning young man, with good abilities and great zeal... I pray God grant him great success in all his undertakings for the good of mankind and a revival of true religion and holiness amongst us in these degenerate days.[67]   *Martin Benson*

In February he went to Bristol and stayed with his sister Elizabeth in Wine Street. He received a huge welcome from members of the religious societies in the city but a cautious one from his fellow clergy. His most controversial action was to speak in the open-air to the colliers at Kingswood, a lawless area in which there was no church:

> 'The poor colliers, who are very numerous, are as sheep having

no shepherd... I went upon a mount and spake to as many people as came unto me... I believe I was never more acceptable to my Master than when I was standing to teach those hearers in the open fields. Some may censure me; but if I thus pleased men, I should not be the servant of Christ.[68]   *George Whitefield*

Hanham Mount became a regular preaching place. This site is commemorated today with a cross

The conditions under which colliers worked were particularly horrendous as a later clergyman who supported Methodism was to make clear:

With what hardships and dangers do our indigent neighbours earn their bread? See those who ransack the bowels of the earth to get the black mineral we burn: how little is their lot preferable to that of the Spanish felons, who work the silver mines?... The murderer's cell is a palace in comparison of the black spot to which they repair; the vagrant's posture in the stocks, is preferable to the posture in which they labour... Form, if you can, an idea of the misery of men kneeling, stooping, or lying on one side, to toil all the day in a confined space, where a child could hardly stand; while a younger company, with their hands and feet on the black, dusty ground, and a chain about their body, creep and drag along, like four-footed beasts, heavy loads of the dirty mineral, through ways almost impassible to the curious observer. [69]   *John William Fletcher*

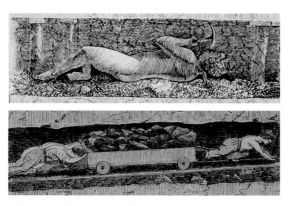

Colliers at work as later depicted in 1842 Royal Commission Report (public domain)

The display on Whitefield as a preacher in the Museum at the New Room

George had got used to preaching in the open air in America and his success at Kingswood led him to begin preaching outside in several places in Bristol. He drew huge crowds which he estimated at times to number over 20,000 people:

He is a born orator... His deep-toned yet clear and melodious voice... is perfect music to listen to... And he speaks so easily, without any apparent effort... It is truly wonderful to see what a spell this preacher often casts over an audience by proclaiming the simplest truths of the Bible. I have seen upwards of a thousand people hang on his words with breathless silence, broken only by an occasional half-suppressed sob. He impresses the ignorant, and, not less, the educated and refined... and few return [from hearing him] unaffected... He speaks from a heart all aglow with love, and pours out a torrent of eloquence which is almost irresistible. [70]   ***Sarah Edwards***

Whitefield had been trained as a child as an actor and he captivated audiences by his ability to tell Biblical stories in a very dynamic way. Each person felt as if he was speaking directly to him or her:

I thought it was all spake to me. [71]   ***Sarah Ibison***

Whitefield met up with Howell Harris, a pioneering open-air evangelist from Wales, and the two men struck up an immediate friendship. This was to be an important link in encouraging early Methodism to accept that preaching could be undertaken by a layman (i.e. a person who is not ordained):

Howell Harris (New Room Archives and Library)

I was much refreshed with the sight of my dear brother Howell Harris... A burning and shining light has he been... [in Wales], a barrier against profaneness and immorality, and an indefatigable promoter of the true Gospel. About three or four years God has inclined him to go about doing good... Twice he has applied (being every way qualified) for Holy Orders, but was refused... He has been made the subject of numbers of sermons, has been threatened with public prosecutions, and had constables sent to apprehend him. But God has blessed him with inflexible courage... and greatly blessed his pious endeavours. Many call and own him their spiritual father... He has established nearly thirty societies in South Wales and still his sphere of action is enlarged daily. He is full of faith.[72]   *George Whitefield*

Whitefield sought to persuade one of his clergyman friends from among the former Oxford Methodist to take on what he had started because he had promised to return to America:

There is a glorious door opened among the colliers. You must come and water what God has enabled me to plant.[73]

George Whitefield

Only John Wesley was prepared to break convention and consider undertaking preaching in the open air. He arrived in Bristol on 29 March 1739:

In the evening I reached Bristol and met Mr Whitefield there. I could scarce reconcile myself at first to this strange way of preaching in the fields, of which he set me an example on Sunday; having been all my life, till very lately, so tenacious of every point relating to decency and order, that I should have thought the saving of souls almost a sin, if it had not been done in a church. In the evening (Mr Whitefield being gone) I began expounding [to the society that met in Nicholas Street on] our Lord's Sermon on the Mount, one pretty remarkable precedent of field preaching. [74]   *John Wesley*

On 2 April John Wesley preached for the first time in the open air in a brickyard in St Philip's Plain in Bristol:

At four in the afternoon I submitted to be more vile, and proclaimed in the highways the glad tidings of salvation, speaking from a little eminence… to about three thousand people. The Scripture on which I spoke was this… 'The Spirit of the Lord is upon me, because he has anointed me to preach the gospel to the poor'. [75]   *John Wesley*

It pleased the Lord to call me out of darkness into his marvellous light… I went out of curiosity and heard that man of God… with astonishment… When the sermon was over I followed him, but knew not why I did so… Mr Wesley went into a house to visit a sick person… I continued to follow Mr Wesley to the house of Mrs Norman… I was invited dirty as I was into… the parlour, where was Mr Whitefield's sister and other ladies. Mr Wesley gave out a hymn. Then all knelt in prayer'.[76]

William Webb

A view of industrial Bristol from Pile Hill in engraving by Heath in Corry's History of Bristol 1816 (Bristol Reference Library)

John's preaching was very noticeably not as good as that of Whitefield and it contained some different emphases, but Whitefield's endorsement of Wesley before he left Bristol ensured many were predisposed towards John and therefore went to hear him:

> I heard… [Mr Whitefield] preach the last sermon at Rosegreen and telling that there was one coming after him whose shoe-laces he was not worthy to unloose. I found that was he who stood by him. I found great love in my heart for him after that.[77]
>
> *Mary Thomas*

John persuaded the religious societies that met in Nicholas Street and Baldwin Street to introduce Moravian-style 'bands' (i.e. small single-sex groups of friends who met regularly to encourage each other's faith) and he said he would meet the band-leaders weekly. He commenced preaching extensively in the open air and, as he grew in confidence, his preaching improved and it seems to have become particularly effective among women:

> I never missed one opportunity, night or day, if I knew where he was to be… Then I knew I never kept one of the commands of God. Then I felt I was in my sins and in a state of damnation. And the more I heard… the more clearer it was to me… [Then eventually] I felt in one moment Christ died for me. I knew my sins were forgiven me… I felt such a peace and love in my heart which no tongue can utter.[78]   *Sarah Colston*

On 12 May 1739 a foundation stone was laid for 'a new room' in which the societies that met in Nicholas Street and Baldwin Street could combine. George Whitefield raised much of the money required and by the autumn the New Room was Wesley's main base:

> We took possession of a piece of ground near St James' churchyard, in the Horsefair, where it was designed to build a

room, large enough to house both the societies... and such of their acquaintance as might design to be present with them, at such times as the Scripture was expounded.[79]   *John Wesley*

Part of the display on the creation of the New Room and nearby Kingswood House in the Museum at the New Room

George Whitefield in London and the growth in opposition to 'the Methodists'

James Hutton in later life (public domain)

In London Whitefield commenced preaching in the open-air to ever-increasing crowds:

They were composed of every description of persons, who, without the slightest attempt at order, assembles, crying 'Hurrah!' with one breath, and with the next bellowing and bursting into tears on account of their sins; some poking each other's ribs, and others shouting 'Hallelujah!'. It was a jumble of extremes of good and evil... Here thieves, prostitutes, fools, people of every class, several men of distinction, a few of the learned, merchants, and numbers of poor people who never had entered a place of worship, assembled in crowds and became godly.[80]   *James Hutton*

But this brought increasing opposition from other clergy. Whitefield's frequent references in his preaching to his time as an Oxford Methodist gave that word great publicity and soon he and any linked with him (like Harris and the Wesleys) were called 'Methodists' by their opponents as a way of labelling them as fanatics:

What is this but an outrage upon common decency and common sense? The height of presumption, confidence and self-sufficiency... [This] outward show of piety... is one undoubted sign of... spiritual pride... It is folly that approaches very near to madness... They are schismatical, in their tendency at least, though not so designed... To pray, preach, and sing psalms in the streets and fields

Rev Dr Joseph Trapp by unknown artist (public domain)

is worse, if possible, than intruding into pulpits by downright violence and breach of the peace... [Religion is made] ridiculous and contemptible... Go not after these imposters and seducers; but shun them as you would the plague.[81] *Rev Dr Joseph Trapp*

None of what Whitefield or John Wesley was doing met with the approval of Charles, who feared a religious revival would be less likely if they offended the Church. Even more opposed was the oldest brother, Samuel Wesley, who was seriously ill and shortly to die. He wrote to John:

For God's sake… banish extemporary expositions and extemporary prayers… You overshoot but Whitefield raves.[82]

Samuel Wesley Jr

Undeterred, John extended his preaching to the area around Bristol.

I look upon all the world as my parish; thus far I mean, that in whatever part of it I am, I judge it meet, right, and my bounden duty to declare unto all that are willing to hear, the glad tidings of salvation. [83]

John Wesley

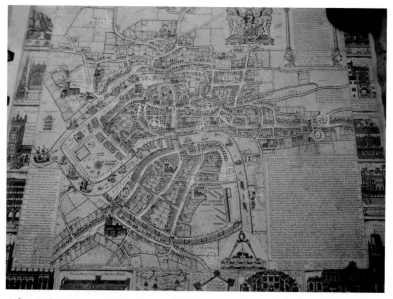

A floor in the Museum at the New Room which depicts the early preaching places used by John Wesley in and around Bristol

A young man from Reading called John Cennick, whom Whitefield had sent to help create a school in Kingswood, preached to the colliers on 17 June when John Wesley was away. Whitefield thought the inexperienced Cennick should not have done this, but Wesley decided to nurture the twenty-one year old Cennick's talent as a preacher. This was the first indicator that John might be prepared to appoint lay preachers to help create a religious revival:

I was sensible of the divine call in my heart, beside the open door before me, but as I had never done such a thing and my conscience was exceedingly tender, I delayed, though persuaded on all sides... We kneeled down simply and asked our Saviour to make manifest his mind... [The answer came] 'To respond'. I stood under a sycamore tree and spoke to several hundreds with a boldness and

John Cennick by unknown artist (Museum of Methodism)

particular freedom in my heart... My preaching was noised over all Kingswood and Bristol so that I could not avoid preaching again.   *John Cennick*

Both John and George Whitefield worked hard to persuade Charles to join them. With Whitefield clearly soon to leave for America, Charles eventually gave in and, on 24 June, commenced open-air preaching in London:

The Lord was with me, even me, his meanest messenger... My load was gone, and all my doubts and scruples. God shone upon my path, and I knew this was his will concerning me.[84]
                                             Charles Wesley

Benjamin Ingham, who has been encouraging the creation of many religious societies in Yorkshire, also commenced preaching in the open air:

> To believe on Jesus Christ is as necessary to salvation as eating
> and drinking is necessary to preserve the natural life... A person

> cannot have the benefit of meat and
> drink, unless he eats and drinks... [and]
> receives the food into his stomach... so
> a man by believing the gospel receives
> Christ and his righteousness into his
> heart, whereby he lives spiritually... He
> feeds on Christ in his heart, or inner man,
> by faith... All that ever have been saved,
> and all that ever shall be saved, have
> been saved and will be saved through
> Jesus Christ and what he has done and

Benjamin Ingham (New Room Archives and Library)

> suffered... Sinners are pardoned on account of the atonement
> made by the blood of Christ. They are redeemed from... eternal
> damnation, the punishment due to their sin. [85]

Benjamin Ingham

In July Whitefield returned to Bristol and was delighted at the progress John had made:

Open-air preaching (Wesley His Own Biographer 1893)

> The people were much
> rejoiced at the news of my
> coming: their hearts seemed
> to leap for joy, and many
> thanksgivings were rendered
> to God on my behalf. The bells were rung unbeknown to me. I
> was received as an angel of God... I found that Bristol had great

reason to bless God for the ministry of Mr John Wesley. The congregations I observed to be much more serious and affected than when I had left them…A great and visible alteration is seen in the behaviour of the colliers. Instead of cursing and swearing, they are heard to sing hymns about the woods; and the rising generation, I hope, will be a generation of Christians.[86]

George Whitefield

In August he embarked for America:

The whole world is now my parish. Wheresoever my Master calls me, I am ready to go and preach His everlasting gospel. My only grief is that I cannot do more for Christ. I ought to love and do much, having had so much forgiven.[87]   *George Whitefield*

Once there, he commenced helping those Americans who wanted to initiate a major religious revival, and his preaching became a major factor in creating what historians now describe as 'the Great Awakening':

In 1739 arrived among us from England the Rev. Mr. Whitefield, who had made himself remarkable there as an itinerant preacher. He was at first permitted to preach in some of our churches; but the clergy taking a dislike to him, soon refused him their pulpits and he was obliged to preach in the fields. The multitudes of all sects and denominations that attended his sermons were enormous and it was [a] matter of speculation to me who was one of the number, to observe the extraordinary influence of his oratory on his hearers, and how much they admired and respected him… It was wonderful to see the change soon made in the manners [behaviour] of our inhabitants; from being thoughtless or indifferent about religion, it seemed as if all the world were growing religious; so that one could not walk through the town in an evening without hearing psalms sung in different families of every street.[88] *Benjamin Franklin*

Benjamin Franklin by Joseph Duplessis 1778 (Harvard Art Museum)

George Whitefield soon became the best known figure in America, helped by huge advance publicity for his preaching tours and by the publication of his writings by Benjamin Franklin, who later became one of the founding fathers of the United States. Though an atheist, Franklin admired Whitefield's talent as an orator and the two men became great friends:

I happened... to attend one of his sermons, in the course of which I perceived he intended to finish with a collection, and I silently resolved he should get nothing from me. I had in my pocket a handful of copper money, three or four silver dollars, and five pistoles [Spanish coins] in gold. As he proceeded I began to soften, and concluded to give the coppers. Another stroke of his oratory made me ashamed of that, and determined me to give the silver; and he finished so admirably, that I emptied my pocket wholly into the collector's dish, gold and all... Some of Mr. Whitefield's enemies affected to suppose that he would apply these collections to his own private emolument [profit]; but I, who was intimately acquainted with him (being employed in printing his sermons and journals, etc.) never had the least suspicion of his integrity, but am to this day decidedly of the opinion that he was in all his conduct a perfectly honest man. And methinks my testimony in his favour ought to have the more weight, as we had no religious connection. He used indeed sometimes to pray for my conversion, but never had the satisfaction of believing that his prayers were heard. Ours was a mere civil friendship, sincere on both sides, and lasted to his death.[89]   *Benjamin Franklin*

3

THE GOSPEL MESSAGE
AS IT WAS PROCLAIMED
AND RECEIVED

John Wesley preaching at Gwennap Pit in Cornwall as depicted in nineteenth-century engraving (New Room Archives and Library)

The religion of love

John and Charles felt they were encouraging people to return to the basics of the Christian faith and to the lifestyle of the early Christians:

> Be rooted in the faith… and grounded in love. [90]
>
> *John Wesley*

Methodist preaching and teaching is sometimes summed up in four statements known as 'the four alls':

1. all need to be saved because of humanity's inherent sinfulness;
2. all can be saved because God's love is open to all;
3. all can have the assurance of knowing that they are saved;
4. all can be saved completely, reaching a state of perfection.

Wesley entering the home of an Irish family (Wesley His Own Biographer 1893)

This message was conveyed not only by preaching in public but also by being willing to engage in individual discussions with people and by incorporating the messages into Charles' hymns. John was very clear about what he hoped to achieve:

You ask, what would I do with them? I would make them virtuous and happy, easy in themselves, and useful to others. Whither would I lead them? To heaven, to God the judge, the lover of all, and to Jesus the mediator of the New Covenant. What religion do I preach? The religion of love. The law of kindness brought to light by the gospel. What is this good for? To make all who receive it enjoy God and themselves, to make them, like God, lovers of all, contented in their lives, and crying out at their death, in calm assurance, 'O grave where is thy victory! Thanks be to God, who giveth me victory, through my Lord Jesus Christ.' [91]   *John Wesley*

John grew increasingly confident that he was undertaking what God wanted because he saw the positive impact of his and Charles' work on the lives of so many people and communities:

God has indeed made bare his arm… in an astonishing a manner among us. This must appear to all who impartially consider it: 1. The number of persons on whom God has wrought; 2. The swiftness of his work in many, convinced and converted in a few days; 3. The depth of it in most of these, changing the heart as well as the conversation; 4. The clearness of it, enabling them boldly to say, 'Thou hast loved me; thou has given thyself to me'; 5. The continuance of it… [even though the revival has been supported only by] two or three inconsiderable clergymen with a few young, raw, unlettered men; and these opposed by well-nigh all the clergy, as well as the laity, in the nation… This is a work of God.[92]   *John Wesley*

Outward observance is not enough

John asserted that all needed to be saved by God because human nature was inherently sinful and no one and no organisation could ensure a person's salvation:

> Even as a child of God... there is a kind of guilt which we are contracting every moment. [93]
>
> *John Wesley*

Going to Church was not enough to acquire salvation. Nor was it sufficient for a person to try and be good and to surround himself or herself with good influences:

> How many of us have said in our hearts, 'O if my lot were but cast among good men and women... I should be free from all these temptations!' Perhaps you would: probably you would not find the same sort of temptations which you have now to encounter. But you would surely meet with temptations of some other kind, which you would find equally hard to bear. For even good men and women... [are] yet are not freed from the remains of sin. [94]
>
> *John Wesley*

Charles powerfully expressed the nature of inbuilt sin in his verse:

> Darkness in my mind,
> perverseness in my will,
> love inordinate and blind,
> which always cleaves to ill;
> every passion's wild excess...
> Show me, as my soul can bear,
> the depth of inbred sin. [95]
>
> *Charles Wesley*

The Methodist approach caused understandable concern to those who had thought attending church or 'being good' was all that was required:

> Having lived almost fifty-five years in this world I found I was ignorant of God. I always thought myself as good as my neighbours and a great deal better than some of them that did curse and swear and got drunk. I always had a good name amongst my acquaintance, which was pleasing to flesh and blood. But the Lord soon showed me that I was a devil and had only deceived myself and all that knew me. When I went to Church I seldom found anything that disturbed me except it was being there too long. But when I came to hear Mr John Wesley I found nothing but discontent in my mind. He told me things that I had said and done when I was a child and from my youth up... so that I had no peace in my mind. [96]   *Mary Thomas*

> Many times by his [i.e. John Wesley] preaching I have been, as it were, sawn asunder, and at my wit's end; not knowing what to do... I found out that what I had done was as nothing, and [I] had not as much begun to be a Christian... and [was] in a sinful state... I was ashamed by my own vileness.[97]   *Naomi Thomas*

> [When it was said] that we deserved to be damned, I thought I might be excepted, thinking I was not so bad as a whore or a drunkard. But soon after I saw that my inward parts were very wickedness and [that I] could put myself on a level with the chief of sinners... When I went to bed I feared I should be in hell before the morning... My conscience... was as the troubled sea that cannot rest... In this state I continued for several weeks.[98]
> *Elisabeth Sayse*

Salvation by faith

John told people what was required to conquer sin and achieve salvation was not some external influence or activity but an entire change of heart:

Seek an inward not an outward change. [99]

John Wesley

John Wesley by John Harley 1745 (Museum of Methodism)

All that was required for that change of heart and a resulting assurance of salvation was that a person should repent of their sinfulness and put their trust in God to forgive them and transform them:

I often said Mr [John] Wesley teaches us an easy way to get… [to Heaven]. He says 'tis but to believe and heavens yours. Glory be to God for his grace.[100]

Elizabeth Downs

Weary of this war within,
weary of this endless strife,
weary of ourselves and sin,
weary of a wretched life,
fain we would on you rely,
cast on you our sin and care. [101]

Charles Wesley

The brothers constantly stressed that the forgiveness of God was only made possible because of the sacrifice made by Christ:

It is through his merits alone that all believers are saved.[102]

John Wesley

If we have not the kingdom of heaven within us, and the earnest of our everlasting inheritance, we are also in the dark and in uncertainty, and are in no better state than those who never heard Christ named... Nothing can satisfy but the whisper of the Redeemer to the heart: 'Your righteousness is of me, I am your salvation'.[103]

John Cennick

Statue of John Wesley on horseback by Arthur George Walker in the Broadmead Courtyard at the New Room

Early Methodists often expressed their amazement at the extent of God's love for humanity, shown in his willingness to permit his son Jesus to face all the horrors of crucifixion. For past, present and future generations, it was Christ's blood that paid the price for sin:

Christian faith is not only an assent to the whole Gospel of Christ but also a full reliance on the blood of Christ...[for] our salvation.[104]

John Wesley

Outcasts of men, to you I call,
harlots, and publicans, and thieves;
he spreads his arms to embrace you all...
Come, O my guilty brethren, come,
groaning beneath your load of sin;
his bleeding heart shall make you room,
his open side shall take you in...
For you the purple current flowed
in pardon from his wounded side,
languished for you the eternal God,
for you the Prince of Glory died.
Believe, and all your sin's forgiven,
only believe and yours is heaven. [105]

Charles Wesley

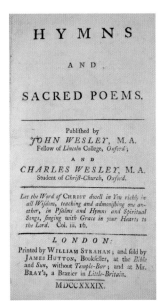

HYMNS

AND

SACRED POEMS.

Publiſhed by
JOHN WESLEY, M.A.
Fellow of *Lincoln* College, *Oxford*;
AND
CHARLES WESLEY, M.A.
Student of *Chriſt-Church, Oxford*.

Let the Word of CHRIST *dwell in You richly in all Wiſdom, teaching and admoniſhing one another, in Pſalms and Hymns and Spiritual Songs, ſinging with Grace in your Hearts to the Lord.* Col. iii. 16.

LONDON:
Printed by WILLIAM STRAHAN; and ſold by JAMES HUTTON, Bookſeller, at the *Bible* and *Sun*, without *Temple-Bar*; and at Mr. BRAY's, a Brazier in *Little-Britain*.

MDCCXXXIX.

Hymns and Sacred Poems 1739 (New Room Archives and Library)

[On the cross] Jesus now cried... with a loud voice: 'It is finished'... that all Hell might hear it, and retreat with shame, having lost their prey, their power and dominion over the souls of men and all right to reign over them for ever... He cried with a loud voice that all sinners might hear it, and know, that now the redemption was finished, an end put to the curse, Satan's head bruised, death destroyed... and its sting taken away, the keys of Hell and the grave delivered into the hands of Jesus, the world redeemed... [and] everlasting righteousness brought in, reconciliation made, pardon obtained, peace proclaimed, and the gate of Heaven opened to all believers. [106]

John Cennick

The sacrifice of Christ had the power to touch the heart of every individual and, when a person gave their heart to Jesus, assurance of salvation followed:

I hunger and thirst after Jesus... I want the blood of Christ every moment applied to my unrenewed soul. I feel I hang upon him for I am weak and helpless... O that I may... ever think I am anything but a poor helpless sinner waiting at the feet of Jesus till his cleansing blood has washed my soul from all sin. [107]

Susanna Designe

Charles Wesley statue by Frederick Brook Hitch in its original location at the New Room.

Amazing love! How can it be
that thou, my God, should die for me?...
He left his Father's throne above,
so free, so infinite his grace,
emptied himself of all but love,
and bled for Adam's helpless race.
'Tis mercy all, immense and free,
for, O my God, it found out me![108]

Charles Wesley

On the path to a holier life

Salvation by faith opened the way to a holier life and set the Christian on the path to perfection. From the outset a born again Christian felt he or she was already living within the Kingdom of God:

Walking in all your ways, we find
our heaven on earth begun. [109]   *Charles Wesley*

John Wesley preaching (Wesley His Own Biographer 1893)

Our main doctrines... are three: that of repentance, of faith, and of holiness. The first of these we account, as it were, the porch of religion; the next, the door; the third, religion itself.[110]   *John Wesley*

For that reason early Methodists often expressed how very upset they were when they failed to live up to their promises. They saw they required constant forgiveness:

> You asked me if I was not troubled with self and pride... [and] I knew not how to answer... I went into mourning for the loss of my Saviour... I was as Noah's dove, and could find no rest till I was again taken into the ark.[111]   *Elisabeth Sayse*

In this situation it was all too easy to fall back into thinking salvation was something to be won:

> He treads the same dreadful round of sin, repenting and sinning again. His comfort is withdrawn, his peace is lost: he prays, resolves, and strives, but all in vain, the more he labours, the less he prevails, the more he struggles, the faster he is bound. [112]
> *Charles Wesley*

That is why Charles often made reference in his hymns to the need for prayerful daily renewal:

> Forth in your name, O Lord, I go,
> my daily labour to pursue;
> you, only you, resolved to know
> in all I think or speak or do. [113]   *Charles Wesley*

Both brothers constantly stressed that salvation by faith required commitment if it was to be fully operative:

> We have to be not almost Christians but altogether Christians.[114]
> *John Wesley*

John Wesley by Nathaniel Hone 1766
(National Portrait Gallery)

The nature of this commitment was threefold: to agree to do no harm and avoid evil of every kind, to agree to undertake works of love according to your means and as often as you could to as many as you could, and, above all, to agree to make use of 'the ordinances of God' (reading the Bible, attending worship, taking communion, praying, and fasting) so you were open to God's grace and the transforming power of the Holy Spirit:

> Love divine, all loves excelling,
> joy of heaven, to earth come down;
> fix in us your humble dwelling;
> all your faithful mercies crown!
>
> Jesus you are all compassion,
> pure, unbounded love thou art;
> visit us with your salvation;
> enter every trembling heart. [115]

Charles Wesley

The resulting transformation in a person's life

Faith in God's transforming grace was central to the thinking of the early Methodists:

> Faith lends its realising light,
> the clouds disperse, the shadows fly,
> the invisible appears in sight,
> and God is seen by mortal eye. [116]   *Charles Wesley*

There is no state of life but needs much grace, and no real happiness but what comes from God... It was powerfully applied to my mind, 'The grace of God and nothing else'. I have ever found it true. Jesus is all in all to the believing soul. [117]

Hannah Ball

God's grace provided believers not just with an assurance that they would go to heaven rather than to hell in the afterlife but also with a new direction to their daily lives:

By salvation I mean not... the vulgar notion [of] deliverance from hell or going to heaven but a present deliverance from sin... the renewal of our souls after the image of God in righteousness and true holiness, in justice, mercy, and truth. [118]   *John Wesley*

I received it in such a manner as I never expected. I felt in my impious soul that I was forgiven; it was like I was flying on the wings of love up to my Saviour's breast. The angel of the Lord came upon me and marvellous light shone into my prison; and my chains fell off. I found that my Saviour was a physician that healed both body and soul... I cannot express the happiness I then enjoyed. [119]   *Elisabeth Sayse*

It totally transformed an individual's views on what it was possible for him or her to achieve:

> All things are possible to him
> that can in Jesus' name believe…
> If nothing is too hard for thee,
> all things are possible to me. [120]
>
> *Charles Wesley*

And gave each Christian an abiding joy:

> My God, I am yours, what a comfort divine,
> what a blessing to know that my Jesus is mine!
> In the heavenly Lamb thrice happy I am,
> and my heart it does dance at the sound of his name. [121]
>
> *Charles Wesley*

Pulpit used by John and Charles in West Street Chapel in London and now in St Giles in the Fields

The Lord awakened me with 'Peace be unto you. Yours sins are forgiven you'. I went home full of joy… I am lost in wonder when I see what God has done for my soul. [122]   *Elizabeth Hinsome*

I felt my heart open within me and like a fountain of water run from it and in that moment I felt such love, peace, and joy past all expression. We sang a hymn and I thought I was out of this body with the angels in heaven for I was full of such joy. [123]   *Thomas Cooper*

A different set of priorities

John and Charles preached that the experience of knowing one was loved by God required a response. Gratitude was best expressed by seeking to make the world a better place:

> He who governed the world before I was born shall take care of it likewise when I am dead. My part is to improve the present moment. [124]   *John Wesley*

Being forgiven should encourage a person to forgive:

> I have often repented of judging too severely, but very seldom of being too merciful. [125]   *John Wesley*

And helping others was the best way of expressing your thanks to God. John and Charles therefore preached that Christians should adopt a lifestyle that was not only productive but also philanthropic:

> Having, first gained all you can, and, secondly saved all you can, then give all you can.[126]   *John Wesley*

Ceramic busts and other memorabilia reflecting the iconic status of John Wesley in the nineteenth century. On display in the Preachers' Room in the Museum at the New Room

Serving others was the best way of growing in your faith:

Miss no opportunity to do good. [127]   *John Wesley*

Finish, then, your new creation,
pure and spotless let us be.
let us see your great salvation
perfectly restored in thee.
Changed from glory into glory,
till in heaven we take our place,
till we cast our crowns before you
lost in wonder, love and praise.[128]

*Charles Wesley by John Russell
(Museum of Methodism)*

Charles Wesley

John preached that Christians might make mistakes or be unsuccessful in their endeavours, but God would judge them not on outcomes but on intentions:

I believe God respects the goodness of the heart rather than the clearness of the head. [129]   *John Wesley*

Wesley preaching. It was usual at meetings for men and women to sit separately (Wesley His Own Biographer 1893)

He also proclaimed that God stood by his followers in order that they should make the best out of all that they faced in life:

Let us receive every trial with calm resignation, and with humble confidence that he who has all power, all wisdom, all mercy, and all faithfulness, will first support us in every temptation, and then deliver us out of all: so that in the end all things shall work together for good. [130]

John Wesley

If a person did not show love to others, then they lacked a true faith:

Love cannot be hid... A secret, unobserved religion cannot be the religion of Jesus Christ. Whatever religion can be concealed is not Christianity. [131]
John Wesley

The Wesleyan message on Christian living was famously summed up:

Do all the good you can,
by all the means you can,
in all the ways you can,
in all the places you can,
at all the times you can,
to all the people you can,
as long as ever you can. [132]
John Wesley

The role of a Christian within the grand scheme of things

John Wesley by William Hamilton 1787 (National Portrait Gallery)

John and Charles did not try to produce answers to every question a person might ask. They preached that many things in life were never going to be fully understood:

Bring me a worm that can comprehend a human, and then I will show you a human that can comprehend God... Who is able to comprehend how God is in this and every place?… What conception can we form of his eternity?… How little do we understand of his providential dealings, either with regard to nations, or families, or individuals?… A full conviction of our own ignorance may teach us a full trust in his wisdom… [and to say] 'Father, not as I will, but as thou will'[133]

John Wesley

Being willing to put one's trust in God, even in the midst of doubts or uncertainties, was therefore essential:

> Let me cast myself aside,
> all that feeds my knowing pride;
> not to man, but God submit,
> lay my reasonings at your feet…
> only seeing in your light,
> only walking in your might. [134]   *Charles Wesley*

So too was having the sense to realise that all Christians needed to know about God was to be found in the life and witness of Christ. Even as an infant, Jesus was God incarnate:

> Our God contracted to a span,
> incomprehensibly made man…
> See in that infant's face
> the depths of deity…
> and we the life of God shall know,
> for God is manifest below. [135]   *Charles Wesley*

The ultimate aim for every Christian was therefore to become as Christ-like as possible:

> A heart in every thought renewed,

and full of love divine,
perfect, and right, and pure, and good,
a copy, Lord, of thine! [136]   *Charles Wesley*

John and Charles were keen to convey that the Christian's focus should not be dwelling on the past or on the future but living in the present:

To serve the present age,
my calling to fulfil;
O may it all my powers engage
to do my Master's will.[137]

Charles Wesley

Statue of Charles Wesley by Frederick Brook Hitch outside the Horsefair entrance to the New Room

---

They and their preachers encouraged people to be aware they could mutually strengthen each other's faith:

Rejoice ye who are partakers of our precious faith, and of the hope full of immortality… Be always examining and trying your faith (as birds try their wings when they prepare to fly)… Be strong, be of one mind as stones firmly built up together in the well tempered mortar of Jesus Christ's blood! See that you walk circumspectly and let the world see you are Christ's disciples because you love one another!' [138]   *John Cennick*

He bid us build each other up
and, gathered into one,
to our high calling's glorious hope
we hand in hand go on.[139]

Charles Wesley

79

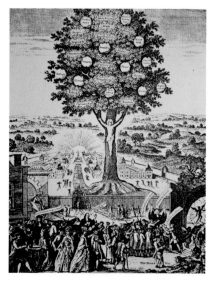

John Wesley and George Whitefield preaching the road to heaven (New Room Archives and Library)

The early Methodists were taught to believe that, whatever joy they experienced as a Christian, it was as nothing to the joys that lay ahead:

As the rivers all return to the sea, so the bodies, the souls, and the good works of the righteous, return to God to live there in his eternal repose. [140]   *John Wesley*

Great things, indeed... has the Lord done... and yet, O stupendous grace! we have only received a drop from the ocean of his love. An endless prospect, and a maze of bliss, lie yet before us! opening beauties, and such lengths, and breadths, and depths, and heights, as thought cannot reach or mind of man conceive! It is, my friend, the fulness of the triune God, in which we bathe, and plunge, and sink, till lost and swallowed up in the ever-increasing, overflowing ocean of delights. [141]

Hester Ann Roe

Early Methodist writings are full of accounts of how dying people calmly endured suffering and pain because of their confident belief that they would next experience the wonders of heaven:

The complaint so affected her throat that she could neither swallow nor speak without great pain... She laboured much to speak and at last said, 'I cannot tell you what sweet communion

I had last night with my Jesus. He seemed very near and loving. I was praising him for all his mercies... O what a comfort! No matter for this body'. She told me she was overcome with the goodness of God... She was such a pattern of patience as I scarcely ever saw and often said with a smile, 'Well, if it will glorify God, I am ready to suffer all this forty years. His will is all in all'... She remained some hours in the pangs of death...[till] her happy spirit took its flight.[142]   *Mary Bosannquet Fletcher*

She went again to the preaching in the evening and stayed for the society meeting, but returned very ill with a pain in her chest... In the night the pain returned again with violence, attended with shivering and cold sweats... We sent for the doctor, who said she was very bad... She began praying for her bands, class, friends, and the church of God, that they might all meet above. Being requested to spare herself, she said, 'My dear, I go now... I know I am going to glory.' A little before she expired, she said to one that was present, ' If I had strength, how could I praise him!'... Without a groan or struggle she closed her eyes and sweetly fell asleep in Jesus. [143]   *Ann Trip*

Charles Wesley thought to be painted by his daughter Sally (Trewint Cottage, Cornwall)

Death was not an end but a new beginning – a time of joining the community of the saints and meeting once more those we have loved and lost :

Come let us join our friends above
that have obtained the prize,
and on the eagle wings of love
to joys celestial rise. [144]

Charles Wesley

4

METHODISM TAKES
SHAPE BUT NOT
WITHOUT DIVISION
1739-42

John Wesley clashes with Beau Nash in Bath (Wesley His Own Biographer 1893)

Growing opposition

Joseph Butler, Bishop of Bristol (New Room Archives and Library)

On 16 August 1739 Joseph Butler, the Bishop of Bristol, expressed his opposition to what John Wesley was doing in Bristol:

Mr. Wesley, I will deal plainly with you. I once thought Mr. Whitefield and you well-meaning men. But I can't think so now. For I have heard more of you – matters of fact, sir... The pretending to extraordinary revelations and gifts of the Holy Ghost is a horrid thing, a very horrid thing. [145]

Joseph Butler

The reason for the Bishop's hostility was that very early on in his preaching John had begun encouraging emotional behaviour in the crowds, such as shrieking and shouting, because he saw it as a sign that the devil was being overcome:

I have seen people so foam and be violently agitated that six men could not hold one, but he would spring out of their arms or off the ground, and tear himself as in hellish agonies. Others I have seen sweat uncommonly and their necks and tongues swell and twist out of all shape. Some prophesied, and some uttered the worst of blasphemies against our Saviour... Oftentimes the same persons were seized and grew intolerable, and though they prayed with them whole nights they were rather worse and worse. [146]

John Wesley

The emotional behaviour increasingly alienated the clergy and the authorities in Bristol:

Lord Jesus's cause constrains me to speak...to cry aloud against these lying dreamers, who cause his people to err and thereby to pervert their ways; these false dissembling hypocrites, who by falling into divers strange postures, and their frightful shrieks and groans, and other ridiculous gestures, would make the world sensible, that the work of conversion is manifestly wrought upon their souls.[147]   *Anonymous letter*

Part of the display in the Museum at the New Room on the opposition to Methodism

Both George Whitefield and Charles Wesley tried in vain to persuade John that encouraging emotional behaviour was unhelpful:

I cannot think it right in you to give so much encouragement to those convulsions which people have been thrown into under your ministry... The devil. I believe, doth interpose. I think it will encourage... people... [to] depend on visions, convulsions, etc more than on the promises and precepts of the gospel.[148]

George Whitefield

That same August there was a court case brought against the Welsh preacher Howell Harris. This was an attempt to stop Methodism on political grounds by saying it was a cover for a subversive movement designed to overthrow the government. When the case collapsed, Harris took it as a sign that God was vindicating the right of chosen laymen to preach:

> O may the Lord fill us all so with His power that we may never rest day or night, but continually go about with our lives in our hands, calling poor sinners to come to Christ, and building the lambs up in Christ. [149]
>
> *Howell Harris*

It was against this background that Beau Nash, as the Master of Ceremonies in fashionable Bath, tried in vain to stop John Wesley preaching:

He asked by what authority I did such things. I answered, 'By the authority of Jesus, my Master, conveyed to me by the (now) Archbishop of Canterbury'. He said it was contrary to the Act of Parliament… against conventicles. I replied, 'The conventicles there mentioned were seditious meetings, but there was no such here'. He said, 'Yes, it was –for I frightened people

Richard Beau Nash by William Hoare
(Tunbridge Wells Museum and Art Gallery)

out of their wits'. I asked if he had ever heard me preach; if not, how could he judge of what he had never heard. He said, 'By common report for he knew my character'. I then asked, 'Pray, sir, are you a justice of the peace, or the mayor of this city?' Answer:

'No, I am not'. W[esley]: 'Why then, sir, by what authority do you ask me these things?...Give me leave, sir, to ask, is not your name Nash?' Answer: 'Sir, my name is Nash'. W[esley]: 'Why then, sir, I trust common report is no good evidence of truth'. Here the laugh turned full against him, so that he looked about and could scarce recover.[150]   *John Wesley*

John moves to London and Charles takes on responsibility for the revival in Bristol

---

Charles Wesley took over the leadership at the New Room in Bristol so John could preach in London:

> We were all of one heart and mind... I felt all at once into the strictest intimacy with these delightful souls, and could not forebear saying, 'It is good for me to be here'.[151] *Charles Wesley*

John and Charles preaching (New Room Archives and Library)

Charles soon established himself as an outstanding preacher and pastor:

I got a guide and went to hear him. I found him standing on a table-board, in an erect posture, with his hands and eyes lifted up to heaven in prayer, surrounded with, I guess, more than a thousand people; some few of them fashionable... but most of the lower rank of mankind... He prayed with uncommon fervency, fluency, and variety of proper expression. He then preached about an hour... in such a manner as I have seldom, if ever, heard any Minister preach... to convince his hearers that... God is willing to be reconciled to all, even the worst of sinners. Although he used no notes, nor had anything in his hand but a Bible, yet he delivered his thoughts in a rich, copious variety of expressions, and with so much propriety that I could not observe anything incoherent, or inaccurate through the whole performance, which he concluded with singing, prayer, and the usual benediction... Never did I see or hear such fervency in the service of God... If there be such a thing as heavenly music upon earth, I heard it there... I do not remember my heart to have been so elevated, either in collegiate, parochial, or private worship, as it was there and then... If, therefore, any inquire... 'Can any good come out of Methodism?' I can only answer... 'Come and see'. [152]   *Joseph Williams*

A preaching house for the colliers was opened in Kingswood and this became the Wesleys' second main base:

Kingswood House (New Room Archives and Library)

The people that in darkness lay, in sin and error's deadly shade, have seen a glorious Gospel day, in Jesu's lovely face displayed... But O the power of grace divine! In hymns we now our voices raise,

loudly in strange hosannas join,
and blasphemies are turned to praise.[153]   *Charles Wesley*

*The pulpit from Kingswood House as it is
preserved today at Kingswood School in Bath*

John Cennick was the first to preach in the new house and he organised a school for the colliers and their children within it in line with what had been promised by Whitefield, who had largely raised the money for the building:

In his preaching and exhorting he was... blessed. He had a very large share in... [effecting] that wonder of grace among the colliers, not only civilising a generation of them who were deemed to be brutal and irreligious, but filling their minds with truth and their very heads with the life and love which is Christ's... notwithstanding all the disadvantages of their condition.[154]   ***Contemporary account***

John and Charles encouraged Cennick to develop his potential as a hymn writer as well as a preacher:

Remember, I am but a child;
a son but lately reconciled;
thee, when I more of grace possess,
in nobler songs my soul shall bless.
While all thy mercies I enjoy,
hymns shall my grateful lips employ;
beneath the shadow of thy wing
I'll gladly wait, and love, and sing.[155]   *John Cennick*

By September there was mounting opposition from the clergy and from the families of those joining the Methodists:

> Christianity flourishes under the cross. None who follow after Christ… [lack] that badge of discipleship. Wives and children are beaten, and turned out of doors… Every Sunday damnation is denounced against all that hear us… Some lose their bread, some their habitations; one suffers stripes, another confinement; and yet we must not call this persecution . Doubtless they will find some other name for it when they do God service by killing us.[156]   ***Charles Wesley***

Selina Hastings, the Countess of Huntingdon, by unknown artist 1770 (National Portrait Gallery)

However, in London there was growing aristocratic interest in the new movement because the evangelically-minded Selina Hastings, Countess of Huntingdon, had started occasionally attending meetings of the Fetter Lane Society. She did so on the recommendation of her sister-in-law Lady Margaret Hastings, who had been impressed by hearing the preaching of Benjamin Ingham in Yorkshire. He and Lady Margaret married in November. The Countess encouraged John and Charles in their work and became an increasing supporter of Methodism:

> I want… [my heart] on fire always, not for self delight, but to spread the gospel from pole to pole.[157]   ***Selina Hastings***

John decided to create his own base in London. In November

he purchased the lease of 'the Foundery', a derelict former gun manufacturing works. This was near to Moorfields, which had been one of the main preaching sites used by Whitefield:

> Two gentlemen, then unknown to me, Mr Ball and Mr Watkins, came and desired me...to preach in a place called the Foundery near Moorfields... I was soon after pressed to take that place into my own hands. Those who were the most earnest therein, lent me the purchase money... Mr Watkins and Mr Ball then delivered me the names of several subscribers, who offered to pay some four, or six or eight shillings a year towards the re-payment of the purchase money and the putting [of] the building into repair. [158]
>
> *John Wesley*

The London Foundery (New Room Archives and Library)

In Bristol the Wesleys entered into a business relationship with the printer Felix Farley, who had become a member at the New Room. John thought education was as important as preaching and Farley began publishing what John and Charles were writing. Over the next few years their publications were to turn Bristol into the biggest publishing centre outside London. The sale of hymn books was to become a major factor in helping fund the growth of Wesleyan Methodism:

> The disorders of our nature have introduced the necessity of education...The end of education... is to restore our rational nature to its proper state...[to] help us discover every false judgement of our minds, and to subdue every wrong passion in our hearts... The bias of nature is set the wrong way: Education is designed to set it right. This, by the grace of God, is to turn the bias from self-will, pride, anger, revenge and the love of the world, to resignation, lowliness, meekness, and the love of God.[159]
>
> *John Wesley*

The collecting box on the door at the Horsefair entrance to John Wesley's Chapel at the New Room

A horrendously severe winter led the Wesleys to use the New Room as the base for a food bank for the poor. Both it and the Foundery increasingly became centres that served the local community as well as acting as bases for religious societies to meet.

I am God's steward to the poor. [160]

John Wesley

The attack on Calvinist theology

Like many clergymen in the eighteenth century, George Whitefield accepted the theological views of the French Protestant reformer, Jean Calvin. Calvin taught that only a few people (the 'elect') were preordained by God to be saved and the rest of humanity was doomed to hellfire. This was an anathema to John and Charles Wesley, who accepted the alternative thinking of the Dutch theologian, Jacobus Arminius, that salvation was open to all and not just a select few:

Jacobus Arminius (New Room Archives and Library)

Call it... by whatever name you please, election, preterition, predestination, or reprobation, it comes in the end to the same thing... by virtue of an eternal, unchangeable, irresistible decree of God, one part of mankind are infallibly saved, and the rest infallibly damned... If this be so, then is all preaching vain. It is needless to them that are elected; for they, whether with preaching or without, will infallibly be saved... and it is useless to them that are not elected, for they cannot possibly be saved... How uncomfortable a thought is this, that thousands and millions of men, without any preceding offence or fault of theirs, are unchangeably doomed to everlasting burnings!... [Yet Jesus] everywhere speaks as if he was willing that all men should be saved. Therefore, to say he was not willing that all men should be saved, is to represent him as a mere hypocrite and dissembler... a gross deceiver of the people.[161]   *John Wesley*

The Wesleys argued that Calvinism encouraged some people to think it did not matter what they thought or did because they were predestined to be either saved or damned:

I was exceedingly pressed to go back to a young woman in Kingswood... I went. She was nineteen or twenty years old; but it seems could not write or read. I found her on the bed, two or three persons holding her. It was a terrible sight. Anguish, horror, and despair, above all description appeared in her pale face. The thousand distortions of her whole body showed how the dogs of hell were gnawing her heart. The shrieks intermixed were scarce to be endured. But her stony eyes could not weep.

She screamed out as soon as words could find their way. 'I am dammed, damned, lost forever. Six days ago you might have helped me. But it is in the past. I am the devil's now. I have given myself to him. His I am. Him I must serve. With him I must go to hell. I will be his. I will serve him. I will go with him to hell. I cannot be saved. I will not be saved. I must, I will be damned.' She then began praying to the devil.[162]   *John Wesley*

In the spring of 1740 the brothers commenced publicly condemning Whitefield's Calvinist theology. This created such opposition within the Foundery that they had to spend most of their time in London. Ironically this meant that in Bristol and Kingswood they had to rely on John Cennick, although he was a Calvinist. In June Cennick was asked to preach at the village of Upton Cheney and the opposition to Methodism by the local clergy and gentry turned violent:

On one day a man and his wife…. [from nearby Hanham] who were alekeepers joined with the men who persecuted us, and both rode their horses through the midst of the concourse beating with the handles of their whips all whom they could reach. Many were rode over, one had his toe crushed by the horse's hoof miserably, others had their faces streaming with blood.   *John Cennick*

In London John and Charles felt they had no option but to exclude a vociferous Calvinist opponent at the Foundery called John Acourt, but the more moderate Calvinists took issue with that decision:

My dear brother, do not act the stiff uncharitable spirit which you condemn in others.[163]   *Howell Harris*

By July anger over John and Charles' attacks on Calvinist thinking had spread to Bristol, largely because Whitefield's sister was unhappy at what was being said about her brother in his absence. The resulting infighting led to the collapse of Charles' health:

> I was taken with a shivering and then the fever came. The next morning I was bled... My pain and disease increased for ten days; so that there was no hope for my life... It was reported I was dead, and published in the papers... [But] God had not finished... his work in me: therefore he held my soul in life; and made all things work for my recovery.[164]   *Charles Wesley*

John Cennick leads the way for the emergence of the lay preachers

Cennick remained loyal and temporarily took over at the New Room, although not all of its members welcomed a layman preaching:

> One night my husband and I were coming to the [New] Room where I expected to hear... [Mr Charles Wesley, but we were told] that Mr Cennick was to be there, at which I was so displeased that I would have returned [home]... had not my husband used his utmost persuasions that I might not. But as soon as I came to the [New] Room I was for going out. But I found at Mr Cennick's giving out of a hymn that I was taking the Enemy's part against my own soul... [and by the end of the service] I went on my way rejoicing.[165]   *Elizabeth Sayse*

The power of Methodism to positively transform attitudes was particularly evident among the colliers in Kingswood. Charles was able to use his influence to prevent a serious riot over the rising cost of corn:

I rode up to a ruffian who was striking one of our colliers [who was refusing to march on Bristol] and prayed him rather to strike me. He would not, he said, for all the world, and was quite overcome. I turned upon one who struck my horse, and he also sunk like a lamb. Wherever I turned, Satan lost ground… [Later] news was brought us that [all] the colliers were returned in peace. They had walked quietly into the city, without sticks or the least violence. A few of the better sort went to the Mayor and told him of their grievances. Then they all returned as they came, without noise or disturbance… Nothing could have more shown the change in them than this. [166]   *Charles Wesley*

Cennick's grandfather had been a refugee from Bohemia and it may have been Cennick's interest in the Moravians that led the Kingswood colliers to hold Moravian-style 'watch-night' services, something that John Wesley then encouraged elsewhere:

I was informed that several persons in Kingswood frequently met together at the school; and, when they could spare the time, spent the greater part of the night in prayer, and praise, and thanksgiving. Some advised me to put an end to this, but, upon weighing the thing thoroughly, and comparing it with the practice of the ancient Christians, I could see no cause to forbid it. Rather, I believed it might be made of more general use. So I sent them word I designed to watch with them on the Friday nearest the full moon, that we might have light thither and back again. I gave public notice of this the Sunday before, and, withal, that I intended to preach; desiring they, and only they, would meet me there, who could do it without prejudice to their business or families. On Friday abundance of people came… and we continued till a little beyond the noon of night, singing, praying, and praising God.[167]   *John Wesley*

Cennick's success encouraged the Wesleys to begin using other lay preachers over the coming months. These included Thomas Westell, Thomas Richards, Joseph Humphreys and Thomas Maxwell – these plus Cennick were to become known as 'the sons of the gospel':

> The word, the care, the labouring zeal,
> he doth to others give,
> and laymen now of Jesus tell,
> and urge us to believe.[168]
>
> *Charles Wesley*

John Nelson (New Room Archives and Library)

Benjamin Ingham also began using lay preachers to support the growing evangelical work in parts of Leicestershire, Yorkshire, Derbyshire, Cheshire and Lancashire. Among the most influential were David Taylor, a servant of the Countess of Huntingdon, John Nelson, a stonemason from Burslem and, by 1742, John Bennet, a packhorse operator from Cheshire. Nelson's faith had been transformed by hearing John Wesley preach in London in 1739:

> As soon as…[Mr Wesley] got upon the stand, he stroked back his hair, and turned his face towards where I stood, and I thought his eyes were fixed upon me. His countenance struck such dread upon me, before I heard him speak, that it made my heart beat like the pendulum of a clock; and, when he did speak, I thought the whole discourse was aimed at me… I believed him to be God's messenger.[169]
>
> *John Nelson*

Using lay men to preach was much condemned and those who took up the role were often portrayed as being either out to make money or madmen. This idea became so prevalent that the writer Tobias Smollett wrote the novel 'Humphrey Clinker' in which a Methodist preacher featured:

Hark ye, Clinker, you are either an hypocritical knave, or a wrong-headed enthusiast; and in either case unfit for service – If you are a quack in sanctity and devotion, you will find it an easy matter to impose upon silly women, and others of crazed understanding, who will contribute lavishly for your support – if you are really seduced by the reveries of a disturbed imagination, the sooner you lose your sense entirely, the better for yourself and the community.[170]   *Tobias Smollett*

Tobias Smollett c1770 by unknown artist (public domain)

The revival suffers from divisions

A Moravian called Philip Molther began to arouse opposition within the Fetter Lane Society to John Wesley's encouragement of emotional behaviour:

The first time I entered the meeting I was alarmed and almost terror-stricken at hearing their sighing and groaning, their whining and howling, which strange proceeding they call the demonstration of the Spirit and of power. [171]   *Philip Molther*

In the spring of 1740 Molther began advocating that the most important thing for a Christian to do was not to follow the activities advocated by the Wesleys but simply to 'be still'. The Wesleys objected strongly:

The chapel in Fetter Lane as it was developed after the Wesleys left (Wesley His Own Biographer 1893)

Many here [i.e. Fetter Lane] insist that a part of their Christian calling is liberty from obeying, not liberty to obey. The unjustified, say they, are to *be still*: that is, not to search the Scriptures, not to pray, not to communicate, not to do good, not to endeavour, not to desire, for it is impossible to use means without trusting in them. Their practice is agreeable to their principles. Lazy and proud themselves, bitter and censorious toward others, they trample upon the ordinances and despise the commands of Christ. [172]   *Charles Wesley*

By June the brothers were no longer welcomed as preachers at the Fetter Lane Society and John took the view that he and Charles should abandon their links with society and the Moravians. The Foundery became the sole base for their work in London, but the divisions within it over the Wesleyan attacks on Calvinist theology made Bristol appear a far more attractive centre:

> O that our London brethren would come to school in Kingswood!
> … Peace, unity, and love are here. [173]   *Charles Wesley*

Those who held Calvinist views placed increasing pressure on John Cennick to break with the Wesleys whilst Charles wrote to Whitefield to reassure him that there was no need for a separation:

Many, I know, desire nothing so much as to see George Whitefield and John Wesley at the head of different parties, as is plain from their truly developed pains to effect it; but be assured, my dearest brother, our heart is as your heart… May you, my brother, and I, especially, be all one, and made perfect in one! When God has taught us mutual forbearance, long-suffering, and love, who knows but He may bring us into exact agreement in all things?… My soul is set upon peace, and drawn out after you, by love stronger than death… You know not how dear you are to me.[174]
Charles Wesley

In November 1740 Cennick begged the Wesleys to stop criticising Whitefield in his absence and, when they ignored him, he refused to continue giving them his public support. Charles wrongly assumed that Cennick had now become their opponent:

You came to Kingswood upon my brother sending for you… You have stolen away the people's hearts from him… God is my witness how condescendingly loving I have been towards you. Yet you did forget yourself, as both openly and privately to contradict my doctrine… Ah, my brother, I am distressed for you.[175]
Charles Wesley

The Wesleyan emphasis on perfection

A significant factor in Cennick's unhappiness had nothing to do with John and Charles' attacks on Calvinism. He had become increasingly annoyed by John Wesley's support for a member at the New Room called Edward Noyers, a Moravian who was claiming he had become totally perfect:

He said he had got so far [in being perfect] that he did not need our Saviour… [and] thought it no robbery to be equal with God. When he said the Lord's Prayer he used to say, 'Forgive *them* their trespasses, etc, and said he never prayed for himself.'[176]

John Cennick

Cennick was happy to strive to lead a perfect Christian lifestyle:

> I want so circumspect to live,
> so free from every sin,
> that e'en the world may perceive
> that I with thee have been.[177]   *John Cennick*

But he thought John was being naive in accepting the perfectionist claims of Edward Noyers and that this was leading others to make false claims:

> [John Wesley] said such sad things in their vindication… [that] we argued hotly and… were both to blame.[178]   *John Cennick*

John Wesley's deep-rooted emphasis on the importance of Christian perfection is often described as Methodism's one distinctive doctrine. John believed that sin lost its power as a consequence of a Christian being saved and reborn to a new life:

> A believer gradually dies to sin, and grows in grace… Use all the grace you have… expect all the grace you want. [179] *John Wesley*

He did not think a Christian's behaviour ever became perfect because all human beings were prone to make errors of judgement and mistakes arising from ignorance and other failings:

> In what sense are Christians not perfect?… They are not perfect

in knowledge... [or] free from ignorance or mistake... They may believe either past or present actions, which were or are evil, to be good... They are not free from... weakness or slowness of understanding, dullness or confusedness of apprehension, incoherency of thought... They are not free from temptation. [180]

John Wesley

But he took the view that Christians could become perfect in intention:

In what sense can Christians become perfect?... [They can] pray without ceasing... be freed from evil thoughts and evil tempers... be purified from pride [and] desire only to do the will of their Father, and to finish his work. [181]   *John Wesley*

Cennick felt that John's theory of perfection was proving counter-productive: it was encouraging some people to think too much about what they were doing and not to rely on salvation by faith and it was creating a divide between those who had the humility to be aware of their continued failings and those who were arrogant and proud enough to claim perfection. Charles Wesley was soon to share that view and he later wrote hymns about how true Christians recognised perfection was only achievable in heaven:

They never boast their grace, or dare
their own perfection to declare,
but still their littleness maintain,
till great in heaven with Christ they reign. [182]

Charles Wesley

The expulsion of John Cennick and the break with the Calvinistic Methodists

Edward Noyers and other perfectionists campaigned against John Cennick. On 24 December John decided to ask Cennick to cease preaching to the Kingswood colliers and in protest Cennick preached nearby:

> I returned early in the morning to Kingswood in order to preach there at the usual hour. But my congregation was gone to hear Mr Cennick so that I had... not above two or three men and as many women. [183]
>
> *John Wesley*

In January 1741 John's attitude furthered hardened when members at the Foundery in London were given copies of a letter written by Cennick asking Whitefield to return to take over the leadership:

> My trouble increases daily. How glorious did the Gospel seem once to flourish in Kingswood! I spake of the everlasting love of Christ with sweet power. But now... it is just as if Satan was now making war with the saints... I believe no atheist can more preach against predestination than they: and all who believe... [in it] are counted enemies of God, and called so... I am as alone... If God give thee leave, make haste. [184] *John Cennick*

Howell Harris from Wales urged that unity be put first:

> I trust our Dear Lord will help us... behave to each other in love... Let us then not quarrel... [When we] meet in love with simple minds, open to the truth, weighing fully what is said on both sides, and praying much, we shall be brought to see we aim at the same things. [185]
>
> *Howell Harris*

On 28 February John formally announced that he was expelling John Cennick from membership:

> He publicly put me out by name, and though I sat with him at the desk, and was a little surprised, yet I showed little of it to the souls, only they saw me weep as I went out, for I said nothing. [186]
>
> *John Cennick*

The revival movement split into Wesleyan Methodists, who followed John and Charles, and Calvinistic Methodists, who, like the preacher Joseph Humphreys, looked instead to Whitefield, Cennick and Harris for leadership. It was a painful break:

> Reverend Sir, I would have been joined with you to all eternity if I could; but ... I now think it is my duty no longer to join with you, but openly renounce your particular doctrines... I feel no bitterness in my spirit, but love you, pray for you, and respect you. [187]
>
> *Joseph Humphreys*

On 15 March George Whitefield arrived back in London from America. Over the coming weeks he tried to reunite Methodism but John Wesley was now set on leading the revival in his own way. This led him, to the dismay of Benjamin Ingham and Charles, to also reject any further co-operation with the Moravians, who were at this stage creating their own separate Church:

> I fear all is not right in your own breast, otherwise you would not think so hardly of them. Is there not envy, self-love, emulation, jealousy? Are you not afraid that they should eclipse your glory, or lessen your own praise ?... I am sure they are a true people of God... I wish we may all love one another – so shall we be disciples of Jesus.[188]
>
> *Charles Wesley*

On 25 April Whitefield arrived in Bristol and once again attracted huge crowds and began changing lives:

Thomas Olivers (New Room Archives and Library)

When the service began, I did little but look about me; but on seeing the tears trickle down the cheeks of some who stood near, I became more attentive... When his sermon began, I was certainly... one of the most profligate and abandoned young men living; but by the time it ended, I was become a new creature... I was deeply convinced of the great goodness of God... I had a far clearer view of my sins... I was filled with an utter abhorrence of my evil ways, and was much ashamed that I had ever walked in them. And as my heart was thus turned from all evil, so it was powerfully inclined to all that is good... I gave myself up to God and his service with my whole heart... [Afterwords] the love I had for Mr Whitefield was inexpressible. I used to follow him as he walked the streets, and could scarce refrain from kissing the very prints of his feet.[189]

Thomas Olivers

Over the next few months Whitefield's preaching ensured that the Calvinistic way of thinking was dominant among the Methodists in Bristol and London and elsewhere. He particularly attacked the 'perfectionists' who had encouraged the Wesleys to get rid of Cennick. However, Whitefield, Cennick, and Harris continued to insist that they had no desire to create a separate organisation and that they wished to be reunited with John and Charles:

May all disputings cease, and each of us talk of nothing but Jesus and Him crucified! This is my resolution. [190] *George Whitefield*

Whitefield made his focus a national preaching tour, including going to Scotland, but John and Charles remained determined to stamp out Calvinist thinking:

> Mercy for *all* thy hands have made,
> immense and unconfined,
> throughout thy every work displayed,
> embracing *all* mankind.[191]   *Charles Wesley*

Only with the benefit of hindsight did Charles feel that he and John should have paid more attention to maintaining unity:

> What dire device did the old serpent find
> to put asunder those whom God had joined?
> From folly and self-opinion rose,
> to sever friends who never yet were foes;
> to baffle and divert our noblest aim,
> confound our pride, and cover us with shame.[192]
>
> *Charles Wesley*

What kept the revival going was the power of Whitefield's preaching. In January 1742 he initiated a major open-air campaign in London and was heartened by the positive response when

Enthusiasm Displayed: a 1739 print of Whitefield preaching and it shows him supported by two women holding masks (one marked 'Hypocrisy' and the other 'Deceit') whilst 'Folly' lies on the ground with a jester's staff and a monkey (New Room Archives and Library)

thousands come to hear him:

> I believe there is such a work begun as neither we nor our fathers
> have heard of. The beginnings are amazing; how unspeakably
> glorious will the end be.[193]
> *George Whitefield*

5
BECOMING
A NATIONWIDE
MOVEMENT
1742-48

John Wesley's multi-purpose chapel was created in the rebuilt and extended New Room in 1748

The Wesleyan class system

Revivals require more than preaching and in February 1742 the 'class' system on which Wesleyan Methodism was to be built was created. This arose entirely by accident when a captain named Foy suggested that the money owed for building the New Room could be paid off if the members formed small neighbourhood groups and these collectively made a weekly contribution. John realised that these groups could become 'classes' in which members' opinions and behaviour could be monitored and controlled by designated leaders:

The class ticket: Methodist 'tickets to heaven' on display in the Museum at the New Room

I was talking with several of the Society in Bristol concerning the means of paying the debts there, when one stood up and said, 'Let every member of the Society pay a penny a week till all are paid'. Another answered, 'But many of them are poor and cannot afford to do it.' 'Then,' said he, 'put eleven of the poorest with me, and if they can give nothing, I will give for them as well as for myself; and each of you call on eleven of your neighbours weekly, receive what they give, and make up what is wanting'... In a while some... informed me they found such and such an one did not live as he ought. It struck me immediately, 'This is the thing, the very thing we have wanted so long.' I called together all the leaders of the classes (so we used to term them and their companies) and desired that each would make a particular enquiry into the behaviour of those whom he saw weekly. They did so. Many disorderly walkers were detected. Some turned from the evil of their ways; some were put away from us.[194]

John Wesley

The Bristol membership class lists in Wesley's handwriting on display in the Museum at the New Room

John and Charles disliked people calling them and their followers 'Methodists' because they feared the Church would think they were trying to create a new sect. John had deliberately given the name 'United Society' to those meeting at the New Room, but this had not prevented the outside world describing it as a Methodist society. Accepting he was stuck with the unwanted word, John chose to define what 'methodism' meant as far as he was concerned:

The distinguishing marks of a Methodist are not his opinions of any sort, his assenting to this or that scheme of religion, his embracing any particular set of notions... A Methodist is... one who 'loves the Lord his God with all his heart, and with all his soul, and with all his mind, and with all his strength'. God is the joy of his heart, and the desire of his soul... He is therefore happy in God... having in him 'a well of water springing up into everlasting life', and overflowing

his soul with peace and joy. Perfect love having now 'cast out fear', he 'rejoices evermore'. He 'rejoices in the Lord always'... having found 'redemption through [Christ's] blood [and] the forgiveness of his sins'.[195]
John Wesley

John Wesley visiting his mother's grave (New Room)

Susanna Wesley before her death in 1742 published a defence of what John and Charles were doing:

I cannot but observe how signally God hath honoured those two brethren... by calling them forth and enabling them with great power to preach the truth of the gospel as it is in Jesus and by setting his seal to their ministry. And I am persuaded you will join with me in prayer to our Lord. That he would strengthen and bless them more and more and protect them from evil men and evil angels, and that they may be steadfast, immovable, always abounding in the work of the Lord. [196]
Susanna Wesley

Methodism and the north

In the spring of 1742 Charles became part of the circle of evangelically-minded clergy that was gathering around Selina Hastings, the Countess of Huntingdon and, at her request, John Wesley copied Whitefield's example and began preaching more widely across the country. In May he headed to the north, travelling through Yorkshire and, encouraged by the stonemason lay preacher, John Nelson, up to Newcastle-upon-Tyne:

> We came to Newcastle… I was surprised: so much drunkenness, cursing, and swearing (even from the mouths of little children) do I never remember to have seen and heard before in so small a compass of time… I walked down to Sandgate, the poorest and most contemptible part of the town; and, standing at the end of the street with John Taylor, began to sing the Hundredth Psalm. Three or four people came out to see what was the matter; who soon increased to four or five hundred. I suppose there might be twelve or fifteen hundred before I had done preaching. [197]
>
> *John Wesley*

The display on John Nelson in the Museum at the New Room. He was later stationed in the Bristol circuit for a year

John's stay in Newcastle was brief so it was Charles who became the true apostle to the north. He proved very successful but also faced strong opposition. Those who were attracted feared they might be persecuted if they supported him:

> [John Wesley] made a great blaze, soon disappeared, and left us in great consternation. Some time after his brother Charles came and preached... I ran with the multitude to hear this strange preacher : when I saw a man in the clergyman's habit, preaching at public place to a large auditory, some gaping, some laughing and some weeping, I wondered what this could mean. When he had concluded, some said, 'He is a good man and is sent to reform our land'; others said, 'Nay, he is come to pervert and deceive us, and we ought to stone him out of our coasts'... I found I was in danger of being called a Methodist and was glad to dismiss the conversation with a smile and a piece of drollery.[198]   ***Christopher Hopper***

John preaching in the Sandgate in Newcastle-upon-Tyne (New Room Archives and Library)

The Calvinistic Methodists had more lay preachers than John and Charles but their quality was very variable:

> I was much surprised to think either Mr Whitefield or any other person should be so weak [as] to encourage such an unqualified man in so awful a work. Such persons as these make religion odious and do more mischief than a thousand persecutors for they betray the cause of Christ to the scorn and contempt and scorn of all its adversaries... 'Tis true Christ's sheep are fools for Christ's sake, but they don't need to make themselves really foolish.[199]
>
> *Contemporary letter*

The best preacher the Calvinistic Methodists possessed after Whitefield and Harris was Cennick. One of the Kingswood colliers who looked to him for spiritual guidance wrote of the change this had made to his assessment of his self-worth:

> I know I am a poor, lost, self-condemned sinner, yet my Master loves me exceedingly... Though I am unfaithful, he is faithful. Though I stray from him, yet He keeps me... I find his grace is sufficient for me in the time of trouble, though I often stand and cannot see which way things will be brought about... He is mine and I am his. I find a closer union to him than ever. Though I am poor, yet in Him I am rich. Though I am despised, yet in Him I am precious. Though I am black, yet I am comely.[200]
>
> *Samuel Tippett*

In July Whitefield embarked on a second tour to Scotland. In contrast to John Wesley, he encouraged the Calvinistic Methodists to work closely with the Moravians. Benjamin Ingham went a step further and decided to join the newly created Moravian Church and hand over all his societies to their control. John Nelson was appalled and he invited John Wesley to take over control of as many societies as possible before the 'German boars' took control of them:

> I am sorry that Mr Ingham should be a tool in their hands... I desired Mr Wesley to write to me... as he was my father in the Gospel.[201] *John Nelson*

The Methodist movement in the north was to be greatly helped over the next twenty years by obtaining the support of the Rev. William Grimshaw, rector of Haworth – a clergyman prepared to travel across huge areas, often on foot, in order to encourage the creation of religious societies:

Rev. William Grimshaw (New Room Archives and Library)

> Many of my hearers who are wicked and careless, are likewise very ignorant, and very slow of apprehension. If they do not understand me, I cannot hope to do them good: and when I think of the uncertainty of life... I know not how to be explicit enough... [Therefore] I express the same thought in different words, and can scarcely tell how to leave off lest I should have omitted something, for the want of which my preaching and their hearing might prove in vain.[202] *William Grimshaw*

Grimshaw's simple preaching was highly effective among those who had little or no education:

> What does the Lord require of you?... Only love and the fruits of love. Love six things and happy you will be for ever. 1. Love the Lord. 2. Love his word. 3. Love his people. 4. Love his ways.

5. Love his works. 6. Love his cross… for truly, what is genuine Christian love but love to God resulting from his love first to you, and shed abroad in your hearts by the Holy Spirit. [203]

William Grimshaw

He produced his own 'methodical' version of daily habits to encourage faith and commitment:

As soon as you awake in the morning, employ half an hour in five things. Bless God for the mercies of the night past; pray for the blessings of a new day; examine well your heart; meditate upon some spiritual subject; and, lastly, plan the business of the approaching day… Rise… [and] while you put on your clothes, praise or pray mentally… Then spend another half-hour on secret meditation, praise, and prayer. After this, call your family together, read a chapter [from the Bible], and, as you have ability… expound it to them; then sing a hymn, and conclude with prayer… [Once you are at work] converse religiously with those about you… As often as you can, retire a few minutes to prayer at nine o'clock in the morning and three in the afternoon. It would be well to spend a little time with your family immediately after dinner. In the evening constantly observe the same order of devotion as in the morning. At going to bed, revise the thoughts, words and actions of the past day. What appears amiss, beg pardon for. What is well, bless God alone for; and never close your eyes to sleep with any unforgiven sin upon your conscience… Do all feelingly, fervently, and devoutly… Custom will make it easy, familiar, and pleasant to you.[204]

William Grimshaw

All who met Grimshaw rated him highly and he and Charles struck up a particularly close friendship:

Rev. Henry Venn by Francis Cotes
1758 (National Portrait Gallery)

[Grimshaw] was only once suspended from his labours by sickness, though he dared all weathers upon the bleak mountains, and used his body with less compassion than a merciful man would his beast... He was like a man with his feet on earth and his soul in heaven.[205]

Henry Venn

The Orphan House in Newcastle (New Room Archives and Library)

In November 1742 John returned to Newcastle to create a centre for Wesleyan Methodism in the north – it was to become known as 'the Orphan House' because it was built to provide facilities for a school for the poor as well as for society meetings and accommodation for visiting preachers:

It being computed that such a house as was proposed could not be finished under seven hundred pounds, many were positive it would never be finished at all; others that I should not live to see it covered. I was of another mind; nothing doubting but, as it was begun for God's sake, He would provide what was needful for the finishing it. [206]

John Wesley

The beginnings of becoming a national organisation

In January 1743 Whitefield reluctantly decided to organise the Calvinistic Methodists because the Wesleys were still refusing to work with him. He created the Anglo-Welsh Calvinistic Methodist Association to run the 36 societies and 25 preaching places that he had across England plus all the societies created by Howell Harris in Wales. It was to have as its central headquarters a temporary building erected near to the Foundery in London. This soon became known as Whitefield's 'Tabernacle'. The Association initiated many things that were to later become a feature of Wesleyan Methodism, such as holding quarterly regional meetings and annual conferences. It also divided lay preachers into two types: those who preached only locally and those who preached further afield, although some local societies objected to losing a good local preacher to the wider itinerant work:

> Brother Cennick we like very well, and should be glad to have him constantly. If you do not take care that we shall have somebody to be with us constantly that we know, and can edify us, you may assure yourself that many in the Society will throw up their tickets.[207]   *John Lewis*

The first Calvinistic Methodist Conference at Watford near Caerphilly (source unknown)

In response John Wesley published 'The Nature, Design and General Rules of the United Societies' to outline the basic structures of his branch of Methodism and its prime aim:

> A company of men... seeking the power of godliness, united in order to pray together, to receive the word of exhortation, and to watch over one another in love, that they may help each other to work out their salvation. *John Wesley*

John Bennet (John Ryland's Library, Manchester)

In April 1743 John Nelson persuaded the talented Calvinist preacher John Bennet to work for the Wesleys rather than Ingham. Bennet had heard and been attracted to Wesley the preceding year:

> I perceived he [Mr Wesley] differed much from Mr Ingham. He was much for working: spoke against waiting on our Saviour – called it a sleepy doctrine... He sent for me to speak with him. I went and he received me courteously. I liked his company.[208] *John Bennet*

Bennet began creating a network of Wesleyan societies across Cheshire and Lancashire:

> Be not wise in your own conceits, lest being puffed up with pride, ye fall under the condemnation of the wicked one. Blessed are the poor in spirit. Blessed are the humble and meek... Desire to be (and by following the humble Jesus, you really will be) little and mean in your own eyes... Seek in fervent prayer, that wisdom which cometh from above which is far from being

earthly, sensual, devilish.[209]   *John Bennet*

In May 1743 John and Charles opened their first Methodist chapel (as distinct from a meeting house) in West Street in the west end of London by leasing a former Huguenot church called Seven Dials. They also introduced a communion service which incorporated hymn singing into it:

> Come Holy Ghost, thine influence shed,
> and realise the sign;
> thy life infuse into the bread,
> thy power into the wine.
> Effectual let the tokens prove,
> and made, by heavenly art,
> fit channels to convey thy love,
> to every faithful heart.[210]   *Charles Wesley*

 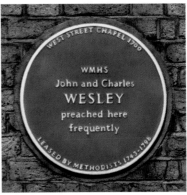

The West Street Chapel in London with the blue plaque that today marks the building's former use by John and Charles

---

The growth in violent opposition

Mounting violence was directed against both branches of Methodism because it was wrongly thought that the Wesleys were secret agents of Bonnie Prince Charlie and therefore part of the Jacobite threat to restore the Stuart line to the throne and so reinstate Catholicism. The belief arose because the Wesleys were known to mix with foreigners and it was easy to portray a religious society meeting as a secret political one. It did not help that it was widely known that their older brother Samuel had been very friendly with a number of the leaders involved in the 1718 Jacobite rebellion:

Bonnie Prince Charlie by Louis Gabriel Blanchet 1738 (National Portrait Gallery)

[They] roared, and shouted, and threw stones incessantly. Many struck, without hurting me. I besought them in calm love to be reconciled to God in Christ. While I was departing, a stream of ruffians was suffered to bear me from the steps. I rose and, having given the blessing, was beat down again. So the third time, when we had returned thanks to God for our salvation. I then, from the steps, bade them depart in peace, and walked quietly through the thickest rioters.[211]

Charles Wesley

John published a defence of what the Methodists were seeking to do:

We see (and who does not?) the numberless follies and miseries of our fellow creatures. We see on every side either men of no religion at all, or men of a lifeless, formal religion. We are grieved at the sight… [and hope to] convince some that there is a better religion to be attained – a religion worthy of the God that gave it. And this we conceive to be no other than love; the love of God and of all mankind... with all our heart, soul, and strength... This love we believe to be the never-failing remedy for all the evils in a disordered world, for all the miseries and vices of men. Wherever this is, there are virtue and happiness going hand in hand... This religion we long to see established in the world, a religion of love and joy and peace... If you are a reasonable man... what is it that you can condemn? What evil have we done to you that you should join the common cry against us? [212]   *John Wesley*

John Wesley facing a mob at Wednesbury 1743 (New Room Archives and Library)

In June Charles undertook a preaching tour of the north. He expressed his continued dislike of John's encouragement of emotional responses from crowds because he thought it encouraged fake reactions:

Many no doubt were, at our first preaching, struck down, both body and soul, into the depth of distress. Their outward affections were easy to be imitated. Many counterfeits I have already detected. Today one who came from the ale-house drunk was pleased to fall into a fit for my entertainment, and beat himself heartily. I thought it a pity to hinder him; so... we left him to recover at his leisure. Another girl, as she began to cry, I ordered to be carried out. Her convulsion was so violent as to take away the use of her limbs, till they laid and left her without the door. Then immediately she found her legs and walked off. Some very unstill sisters, who always took care to stand near me, and try which should cry loudest, since I had them removed out of my sight, have been as quiet as lambs. [213]   *Charles Wesley*

In July Charles Wesley took Wesleyan Methodism into Cornwall following an invitation from a sea captain called Joseph Turner, who had founded a religious society in St Ives. John Wesley followed him there in August:

An army of rebels broke in upon us... They began in a most outrageous manner, threatening to murder the people, if they did not get out that moment. They broke the sconces, dashed the windows in pieces, tore away the shutters, benches, poor-box, and all but the stone walls... Several times they lifted up their hands and clubs to strike me; but a stronger arm restrained them. They beat and dragged the women about, particularly one of great age, and trampled on them without mercy... I bade the people stand still and see the salvation of God... [and] the ruffians fell to quarrelling among themselves.[214] *Charles Wesley*

On 20 October 1743 John was almost killed by a mob at Wednesbury in the midlands:

To attempt speaking was vain, for the noise on every side was like the roaring of the sea. So they dragged me along... from one end of the town to the other... At the west end of the town, seeing a door half open, I made toward it, and would have gone in, but a gentleman in the shop would not suffer me, saying they would pull the house to the ground. However, I stood at the door and asked, 'Are you wiling to hear me speak?' Many cried out, 'No, no! knock his brains out; down with him; kill him at once'... I broke out loud in prayer... A lusty man just behind struck at me several times with a large oaken stick; with which, if he had struck me once on the back part of my head, it would have saved me all further trouble. But every time the blow was turned aside, I know not how.[215]   *John Wesley*

That autumn Charles produced a hymnbook entitled 'Hymns for the Time of Trouble':

> Ye servants of God, your Master proclaim,
> and publish abroad his wonderful name;
> the name all-victorious of Jesus extol;
> His kingdom is glorious, and rules over all. [216]

Charles Wesley

A preacher was always accompanied by at least one companion because of the dangers involved in travelling (Wesley His Own Biographer 1893)

The work of the two branches of Methodism meant it had become a nationwide movement by the end of 1743:

There are few or no counties in England or Wales where there is not a work begun.[217] *John Symns*

*Attack on Quaker use of women as preachers
(public domain)*

In February 1744 Sarah Perrin, arguably the first female Methodist preacher, was appointed as housekeeper at the New Room. As a former Quaker Sarah had experienced women preaching:

I have no party to promote but love unfeigned, no faith to set up but faith in our Lord Jesus, and no religion to press them to but holiness of heart.'[218] *Sarah Perrin*

In Yorkshire Charles was charged with treason and nationwide the threat of a possible Jacobite invasion caused the violence against the Methodists to grow in intensity:

A great multitude… broke down the houses of the Methodists, broke open their boxes, chests, etc and carried away their household stuff… They abused the women with all barbarity and immodesty; they tied ropes about some of the men and dragged them as they pleased; they tied a rope about a boy's neck and afterwards held him up by his ears, while others pelted him, etc, stripping them of their wearing apparel… [so that] parents and children wandered thus naked about the fields… [They set] papers on posts… that they would root out all the cursed Methodists from the country.[219]   *Howell Harris*

In April 1744 the Calvinistic Methodist Association met in Wiltshire and insisted that Cennick should take over when Whitefield returned to America. The violence facing Methodism encouraged those in attendance to also assert their willingness to preach to Wesleyan societies and to permit Wesleyan preachers to preach to their societies:

> We think ourselves in no ways bound to refrain from going to any place where we believe we are called by the Holy Ghost... [and] we think it just on their side that they have the same liberty. [220]   *George Whitefield and John Cennick*

In June the first Wesleyan Methodist Conference was held at the Foundery. It lasted six days and was attended by six clergy and four lay preachers. It defined the aims and roles of preachers, society stewards, and class-leaders:

> I desired my brother and a few other clergymen to meet me in London, to consider how we should proceed to save our own souls and those who heard us. After some time, I invited the lay preachers that were in the house to meet with us. We conferred together for several days and were much comforted and strengthened thereby. [221]   *John Wesley*

The first Wesleyan Methodist Conference in London in 1744 (New Room Archives and Library)

Coping with the Jacobite invasion

In August George Whitefield departed for America, leaving John Cennick in charge in England and Howell Harris in Wales. Once in America, Whitefield engaged on extensive preaching tours across the colonies again:

> God daily blesses my poor labours, I think it is my duty to comply with the invitations that are sent me... To preach the unsearchable riches of Christ... is my meat and drink. [222]

George Whitefield

Whitefield preaching in America (public domain)

In the early part of 1745 Charles' health was so poor that John had to undertake most of the itinerant preaching. He found that the conflict between the two branches of Methodism had noticeably reduced in Bristol as a consequence of the persecution both branches faced:

> I found peculiar reason to praise God for the state of the society, both in Kingswood and Bristol. They seem at last clearly delivered from all vain jangling, from idle controversies and strife of words.[223]

John Wesley

In August the second Wesleyan Methodist Conference was held at the New Room in Bristol with five clergy and six lay preachers:

> You have nothing to do but to save souls. Therefore spend and be spent in this work.[224]
> *John Wesley*

On 21 September Bonnie Prince Charlie's army defeated the British army at Prestonpans and thus opened the way for an invasion of England. This caused panic and intensified the anti-Methodist hostility. John expressed his belief that God was punishing the army and the nation for its wickedness:

> My soul has been pained day by day, even in walking the streets of Newcastle, at the senseless, shameless wickedness, the ignorant profaneness, of the poor men to whom our lives are entrusted. The continual cursing and swearing, the wanton blasphemy of the soldiers in general, must needs be a torture to the sober ear, whether of a Christian or an honest infidel. Can any that either fear God, or love their neighbour, hear this without concern? … For can it be that God should be on their side who are daily affronting him to his face? And if God be not on their side, how little will either their number, or courage, or strength avail?[225]
> *John Wesley*

In December 1745 John Cennick resigned as leader of the Calvinistic Methodists because he was tired of the in-fighting taking place. Like Ingham before him, he sought to join the Moravian Church. His defection was followed by many societies, seriously weakening the Calvinistic branch of Methodism. Only Howell Harris was left to provide any effective leadership for it. When he heard the news in America, Whitefield was very understanding towards Cennick's decision:

My dear John... whether I see thee or not, whether thou dost ever think of me or write to me anymore, I wish thee much success, and shall always pray that the work of the Lord may prosper in thy hands... May Jesus... hasten that blessed time when we shall all see eye to eye, and there shall be no disputing about houses, doctrine or discipline.[226]   *George Whitefield*

The Moravians were very keen to have their new Church recognised by the Church of England and so were not interested in running religious societies lest that offend its hierarchy. They preferred to put their efforts into creating a few Moravians settlements in England. This meant that the societies handed over to them by Ingham and Cennick were forced to turn increasingly to either Wesleyan or Calvinistic Methodist preachers for support:

We wish for nothing more than that some time or other there might be some Bishop or parish minister found of the English Church, to whom, with convenience, and to the good liking of all sides, we could deliver the care of those persons of the English church who have given themselves to our care. [227]

Nicholas von Zinzendorf

The Battle of Culloden on April 1746 ended the Jacobite Rebellion. Hearing the news, Charles held celebrations at the New Room in Bristol:

All their strength o'erturn, o'erthrow,
snap their spears, and break their swords.
Let the daring rebels know
the battle is the Lord's![228]

Charles Wesley

The Battle of Culloden by David Morier 1746 (British Museum)

Methodism continues to expand

The violence towards the Methodists was still to remain a problem for a few more years but this proved no deterrent to the growth of the movement, especially as it was agreed that the two branches of Methodism should work together:

> We all agreed that, if we occasionally preached among each other's people, we should endeavour to strengthen and not weaken each other's hands, and prevent any separation in the several societies... [and it was agreed] we should, on each side, be careful to defend each other's characters. [229]
>
> *Minutes of Conference*

In May 1746 the third Annual Conference was held at the New Room with only three clergy and three lay preachers in attendance because of the difficulties in travelling. It was agreed to divide the Wesleyan Methodist societies into seven huge 'circuits' and to draw up quarterly preaching plans for each circuit. Over the coming years the number of circuits and preachers was to increase. The first recorded formal commissioning of a lay preacher, Jospeh Cownley, took place:

Charles Atmore (New Room Archives and Library)

He was a man of eminent piety, strong sense, and remarkable seriousness... [He] was possessed of a fund of divine knowledge, so that there was a rich diversity in all his discourses... It was generally remarked, 'Mr Cownley has always something new'. Indeed the pulpit was his element and there he shone!... Mr Wesley did not hesitate to say, 'He is one of the best preachers in England'.[230]

Charles Atmore

The renewal of itinerancy led to a growing confidence that a religious revival was taking place:

> The whole country finds the benefit of the Gospel. Hundreds who follow not with us, have broke off their sins, and are outwardly reformed... For one preacher they cut off, twenty spring up. Neither persuasions nor threatening, flattery nor violence, dungeons or sufferings of various kinds, can conquer them. Many waters cannot quench this little spark which the Lord hath kindled, neither shall the floods of persecution drown it.[231]
>
> *Charles Wesley*

In November 1746 Charles celebrated the success of the Methodists in Newcastle and the north, despite the persecution they had faced during the Jacobite rebellion:

> See how great a flame aspires,
> kindled by a spark of grace.
> Jesu's love the nation fires,
> sets the kingdoms on ablaze.
> To bring fire on earth He came,

kindled in some hearts it is;
O that all might catch the flame,
all partake the glorious bliss![232]   *Charles Wesley*

Education and new facilities for the growing movement

John felt the future of the revival rested with the next generation and he and Charles took a genuine interest in encouraging the faith of children, to the extent that Charles was the first person to try and produce hymns specifically for them:

Gentle Jesus, meek and mild,
look upon a little child;
pity my simplicity,
suffer me to come to Thee.[233]   *Charles Wesley*

Giving children the right kind of education was seen as being vitally important:

What is commonly called a religious education frequently does more hurt than good... [giving] children an enmity to religion, which usually continues all their lives... Those that educate them... [about] religion... may be mistaken with regard to the manner of instilling it in children... if they either give children too much of their own will, or needlessly... [use] more punishment than is necessary... Religion will stink in the nostrils of those that were so educated... [Rooting out evil as far as possible should] be done by mildness, softness and gentleness... But sometimes these methods will not avail, and then we must correct with kind severity.[234]   *John Wesley*

In 1747 John started to build a model Christian school for the children of his friends. It was erected alongside the preaching house in Kingswood, probably with financial help from the Countess of Huntingdon. The new Kingswood School opened on Midsummer's Day 1748 and Charles wrote a hymn for the occasion:

> Error and ignorance remove,
> their blindness both of heart and mind;
> give them the wisdom from above,
> spotless, and peaceable, and kind;
> in knowledge pure their minds renew,
> and store with thoughts divinely true…
> Unite the pair so oft disjoined,
> knowledge and vital piety;
> learning and holiness combined,
> and truth and love. [235]
>   *Charles Wesley*

John Wesley walking in grounds of Kingswood School with one of its chief masters many years after its creation (New Room Archives and Library)

John was keen that the teachers should take a real interest in their pupils:

> Beware you be not swallowed up in books. An ounce of love is worth a pound of knowledge.[236]
>   *John Wesley*

And, although much of the teaching was based on rote-learning (as was the norm in the eighteenth century), Wesley recognised the importance of encouraging a true understanding:

> Beware of that common, but accursed, way of making children parrots, instead of Christians. Labour that, as far as possible, they may understand every single sentence which they read... Regard not how much, but how well, to what good purpose, they read... and question them continually on every point... By this means they will learn to think as they read: they will grow wiser and better every day... [and] grow in grace, in the knowledge of God, and of our Lord Jesus Christ.[237]   *John Wesley*

Part of the display on education at the Museum at the New Room

Secretly Kingswood School was also designed to act as a training school for the Methodist lay preachers:

> My design was to have as many of our preachers here... as could possibly be spared and to read lectures to them every day, as I did my pupils in Oxford. [238]   *John Wesley*

In February 1748 John decided to rebuild the New Room, doubling its size and providing rooms for himself and visiting preachers. He had its main hall licensed for worship and it became known as 'John Wesley's Chapel':

> I met about sixty of the society in Bristol to consult upon enlarging the Room; and indeed securing it, for there was no small danger of its falling upon our heads. In two or three days two hundred and thirty pounds were subscribed. We immediately procured experienced builders to make an estimate of the expense. And I appointed five Stewards (besides those of the society) to superintend the work.[239]   *John Wesley*

John Wesley's Rooms now part of the Museum at the New Room

6
METHODISM
AND
SOCIAL JUSTICE

'Gin Lane' engraving by William Hogarth 1751 (New Room Archives and Library)

Loving your neighbour

John and Charles constantly stressed the importance of fulfilling Christ's commandment to love each other:

> Jesus, I fain would find
> Thy zeal for God in me,
> the yearning pity for mankind,
> thy burning charity. [240]
>
> *Charles Wesley*

It is worth quoting in this context John's definition of what it meant to be a true Christian:

> He is full of love to his neighbour, of universal love, not confined to one sect or party, not restrained to those who agree with him or his opinions, or in outward modes of worship, or to those who are allied to him by blood or recommended by nearness of place. Neither does he love only those who love him or that are endeared to him by intimacy of acquaintance... [His love] soars above all these scanty bounds, embracing neighbours and strangers, friends and enemies, yea, not only the good and gentle, but also the forward, the evil, and the unthankful. For he loves every soul that God has made, every child of man, of whatever place or nation... And this universal, disinterested love is productive of... gentleness, tenderness, sweetness, of humanity, courtesy, and affability.[241]
>
> *John Wesley*

Working in cities like Bristol, London and Newcastle, and constantly travelling across the country, made the brothers well aware of the appalling conditions in which many lived, despite the country's great wealth:

'I have seen wretched creatures… standing in the streets with pale looks, hollow eyes, and meagre limbs, or creeping up and down like walking shadows… I have [seen a person]… gathering the bones which the dogs had left in the streets, and making broth of them to prolong a wretched life… Such is the case at this day of multitudes of people in a land flowing, as it were, with milk and honey! abounding with all the necessaries, the conveniences, the superfluities of life!'[242]   *John Wesley*

Sketch showing family suffering from poverty 1799 (public domain)

Part of their response was to create food and clothes banks at their main centres of work and to collect money which could be used to help people:

I reminded the United Society that many of our brethren and sisters had not needful food; many were destitute of convenient clothing; many were out of business, and that without their own fault; and many were sick and ready to perish… I desired all whose hearts were as my heart:1. to bring what clothes each could spare, to be distributed among those that wanted most; 2. to give weekly a penny, or what they could afford, for the relief of the poor and sick.[243]   *John Wesley*

On occasion John also provided temporary work schemes for the unemployed:

> Our aim was, with as little expense as possible. to keep them at once from want and from idleness; in order to which we took twelve of the poorest, and a teacher, into the society room, where they were employed for four months, till spring came on, in carding and spinning of cotton… [and] they were employed and maintained with very little more than the produce of their own labour. [244]
>
> *John Wesley*

Describing himself as God's steward to the poor, John felt it was his prophetic role to remind the rich of the folly of ignoring Christ's commands:

> You know that in seeking happiness from riches, you are only striving to drink out of empty cups. And let them be painted and gilded ever so finely, they are empty still.[245]
>
> *John Wesley*

Two eighteenth-century mezzotints on the transitory nature of human vanity after Robert Dighton's 'An Essay on Man' and 'An Essay on Woman' (New Room Archives and Library)

He frequently encouraged those who were better off to live as simply as possible so they had more money available to help others:

> Cut off all this expense! Despise delicacy and variety, and be content with what plain nature requires... Waste no part of it in curiously adorning your houses; in superfluous or expensive furniture; in costly pictures, painting, gilding, books; in elegant rather than useful gardens. [246]   *John Wesley*

> Do you not know that God entrusted you with that money (all above what buys necessities for your families) to feed the hungry, to clothe the naked, to help the stranger, the widow, the fatherless; and, indeed, as far as it will go, to relieve the wants of all mankind? How can you, how dare you, defraud the Lord, by applying it to any other purpose?[247]   *John Wesley*

A room in the Museum at the New Room which reflects on the deep divisions between the lifestyles of the rich and poor that Wesley opposed

Towards the end of his life John Wesley promoted the Strangers' Friend Society, which was dedicated to raising money to help poor, sick and friendless strangers:

One of the most prominent characteristics [of Christianity] is charity… It engages the best feelings of the heart in the cause of mercy; it directs the footsteps of the beneficent to the hovel of the wretched, the chamber of the diseased, and the bed of the dying; it rears, as the fruits of its benevolence, asylums for the blind, the deaf and the dumb – hospitals for the sick, the maimed and the dying – refuges for the orphan and the destitute – almshouses for the aged and the infirm, and schools for the ignorant.[248]   *Contemporary account*

The brothers believed giving money or gifts was not enough. It was important for Christians to give of their personal time to help others so that the whole atmosphere within local communities changed:

One of the principal rules of religion is to lose no occasion of serving God. And… we are to serve him in our neighbour, which he receives as if done to himself.[249]   *John Wesley*

What an individual could achieve was dramatically increased if he or she also worked alongside other Christians:

Mr. Wesley's people think that they cannot love their neighbour as themselves without endeavouring to find out every possible way by which they may be serviceable to the souls and bodies of their fellow-creatures. In London and Bristol, and I believe in other places, some of their society… endeavour to find out poor, distressed objects who are confined to their beds by diseases in poorhouses, prisons, lodging-houses, dirty lanes, alleys,etc. These poor, forsaken outcasts of society they instruct, exhort, pray with, etc. To objects most in want they give money. Perhaps there cannot be any labour of love more praiseworthy, or more deserving of encouragement, as great numbers of such poor, destitute wretches may at all times be found languishing in a forlorn state, and generally die without anyone caring for them: for none but such as are filled with the love of God and man will ever go into such places and habitations... I have witnessed their cheerful performance of this great duty... No labour, however disagreeable or hazardous to health or life, is too much to be performed by such as are thoroughly impressed with the worth of an immortal soul... Those people, when employed in such work as this, which to flesh and blood is not only irksome but shocking, yet would not have exchanged the pleasure which they found in it for any earthly enjoyment".[250] *James Lackington*

Tackling the needs of specific groups

At varying times John tried to tackle the needs of specific groups. So, for example, he created homes for widows next to the Foundery:

Many, although not sick, were unable to provide for themselves... We took a lease of two little houses near; we fitted them up to be warm and clean. We took in as many widows as we had room for, and provided them with things needful for the body... I myself, as well as the other preachers who are in town, diet with the poor on the same food and at the same table. And we rejoice herein as a comfortable earnest of our eating bread together in our Father's Kingdom.[251]   *John Wesley*

And, in addition to creating Kingswood School, which was his biggest educational project, he set up a number of free schools for the children of the poor and for adults so they could receive an education that might help them better themselves:

It is proposed... to teach chiefly the poorer children to

read, write, and cast accounts; but more especially (by God's assistance) to know God and Jesus Christ... The older people, being not so proper to be mixed with children (for we expect scholars of all ages, some of them grey-headed) will be taught in the inner rooms, either early in the morning or late at night so their work may not be hindered.[252]   *John Wesley*

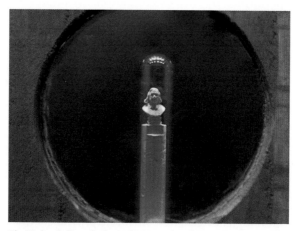

The Wesley chalk on display in the Museum at the New Room. Carved by a teenage boy from Brazil in 1998 to commemorate 250 years after the opening of Kingswood School, Wesley's biggest educational project

John organised teams of visitors to the sick and dying and he created free medical dispensaries in all three main centres of his work:

I gave notice... that all who were ill of chronical distempers (for I did not dare venture upon acute) might, if they pleased, come to me at such a time, and I would give them the best advice I could, and the best medicines I had. Many came... I did not regard whether they were of the society or not. [253] *John Wesley*

Our number of patients increases here daily. We have now upwards of two hundred. Many have already desired to return thanks, having found a considerable change for the better already.[254]   *John Wesley*

John Wesley offering medicine to those who could not afford it (Wesley His Own Biographer 1893)

A bound copy of Primitive Physic in New Room Archives and Library

John quickly ran out of money for the medical dispensaries so he produced a medical self-help guide called 'Primitive Physic' in 1748. It became a best-seller, selling over a million copies over the next hundred years. Although many of its remedies were very much a product of the limited medical knowledge available in the eighteenth-century, the book was remarkable because of its emphasis on measures to prevent illness. One measure, which John repeatedly urged, was the importance of cleanliness:

Avoid all nastiness, dirt, slovenliness, both in your person, clothes, house, and all about you. Do not stink... Mend your clothes or I shall never expect you to mend your lives. Let none see a ragged Methodist.[255]

John Wesley

Display on John Wesley's medical ideas and his focus on well-being in the Museum at the New Room

And he was a strong advocate of adopting a lifestyle that would help keep a person fit and healthy:

Take always… food as sits light and easy upon the stomach. All pickled, or smoked, or salted food, and all high-seasoned, is unwholesome… Water is the wholesomest of all drinks… Strong, and more especially spiritous liquors, are a certain, though slow, poison… A due degree of exercise is indispensable to health and long life. [256] *John Wesley*

When 'Primitive Physic' came under attack from some doctors, John defended its contents with wit:

I do not know that any one patient has yet died under my hands. If any person does, let him now declare it, with the time and circumstances. [257] *John Wesley*

Statue of James Rouquet in the Museum at the New Room

He and Charles regularly visited prisons and they encouraged Methodists to do the same and to campaign for better conditions. The Methodist James Rouquet was a notable example of this in Bristol, not only ensuring the reform of prison conditions but also encouraging schemes to help secure the release of those who were in prison for debt :

> For near twenty years I have… promoted the relief and discharge
> of prisoners… [and] of some hundreds of prisoners who have
> been set at liberty during that period not more than 6 or 8 have
> been imprisoned a second time… [Their release] has proved
> a real advantage to society as well as comfort to themselves.[258]
>
> *James Rouquet*

John's interest in prisons also extended to helping those sent to
lunatic asylums, because often the conditions for those judged
insane were even worse. John rejoiced when he found a Methodist
called James Henderson trying out kinder techniques:

> I am persuaded there is not such another house for lunatics
> in the three kingdoms. He has a particular art of governing
> patients; not by fear, but by love. The consequence is many of
> them speedily recover, and love him ever after. [259]   *John Wesley*

*John Wesley visiting prisoners some of whom are mentally ill
(Wesley His Own Biographer 1893)*

Longer term solutions

John and Charles Wesley are often portrayed as being politically conservative, partly because they believed in the divine right of kings to rule, and partly because they usually avoided getting embroiled in politics. They thought a religious revival offered a far better way of improving society than anything that might be done by a government. Wesley's advice to those who had the vote was very measured:

> I met those of our society who had votes in the ensuing election, and advised them:
> 1. to vote, without fee or reward, for the person they judged most worthy;
> 2. to speak no evil of the person they voted against; and
> 3. to take care their spirits were not sharpened against those that voted on the other side. [260]
>
> *John Wesley*

The audience at a play as depicted in a print of an engraving by Hogarth (New Room Archives and Library)

However, John did lobby parliament over a number of national issues. He attacked the agricultural monopolies that artificially kept food prices high because he knew workers' wages were not keeping pace with food costs. He thought the price of meat could be cut by developing better breeds of cattle and sheep, the price of oats reduced by banning the nobility's excessive keeping of horses, and the price of wheat lowered by banning its use in distilling. He also recommended that less money should be spent on maintaining military and naval forces so that more could be spent on helping the poor and disadvantaged.

Occasionally he could also be quite outspoken on local issues. A good example is his attempt to persuade Bristol not to build a theatre on the grounds it would prove a corrupting influence:

> Most of the present stage entertainments sap the foundation of all religion, as they naturally tend to efface all traces of piety and seriousness out of the minds of men... [and] they are peculiarly hurtful to a trading city, giving a wrong turn to youth...being directly opposite to the spirit of industry and close application to business... Drinking and debauchery of every kind are constant attendants on these entertainments, with indolence, effeminacy, and idleness, which affect trade in an high degree.'[261]
>
> *John Wesley*

Often John Wesley was quite radical in his thinking. So, for example, he attacked a consumerist society that put profit before people and he spoke of the importance of a living wage for workers because many who worked still could not afford to feed and clothe their families:

Part of the display on Wesley's radical agenda in the Museum at the New Room

How many are there in this Christian country that toil, and labour, and sweat… but struggle with weariness and hunger together? Is it not worse for one, after a hard days labour, to come back to a poor, cold, dirty, uncomfortable lodging, and to find there not even the food which is needful to repair his wasted strength?'[262]   *John Wesley*

John campaigned against the view that poor people were 'unworthy':

I love the poor; in many of them I find pure, serious grace, unmixed with paint, folly, and affectation.[263]   *John Wesley*

And he condemned the lack of awareness among the wealthy:

One great reason why the rich, in general, have so little sympathy for the poor, is, because they so seldom visit them. Hence it is, that, according to the common observation, one part of the world does not know what the other suffers. Many of them do not know, because they do not care to know: they keep out of the way of knowing it; and then plead their voluntary ignorances an excuse for their hardness of heart.[264]   *John Wesley*

He repeatedly said how vital it was to try and have full employment and he created funds to lend people money to set up businesses if they had an idea that he thought would work and if they showed the right degree of commitment:

It is impossible for an idle man to be a good man… Without industry we are fit neither for this world nor the world to come.[265]   *John Wesley*

Both brothers encouraged employers to treat their workforce well.

> Brethren in our Creator's eyes,
> I dare not injure or despise
> the workmanship of God. [266]
>
> *Charles Wesley*

John also urged men to view women more as equals, encouraging women to take on leadership roles:

Statue of Sarah Ryan, housekeeper at the New Room, within its Museum – she was one of the many women to whom Wesley gave an important role, despite opposition from those who felt her unsuitable

'There is neither male nor female in Christ Jesus'... It has long passed for a maxim that 'women should be seen, not heard' and accordingly many are brought up in such a manner as if they were only designed for agreeable playthings! But is this doing honour to the sex? Or is it a real kindness to them? No, it is the deepest unkindness; it is horrid cruelty... And I know not how any woman of sense and spirit can submit to it. Let all you [women] that have it in your power assert the right which the God of nature has given you. Yield not to that vile bondage any longer! You, as well as men, are rational creatures. You, like them, were made in the image of God; you are equally candidates for immortality; you too are called of God.[267]

John Wesley

In age of immense cruelty to animals, John laid down rules as to how his preachers should look after their horses and he also argued for the better treatment of all animals:

If the Creator and Father of every living thing... does not overlook or despise any of the works of his own hands... how comes it to pass, that such a complication of evils oppresses, yea, overwhelms them... Pain is an experience that is unpleasant for all animals, human and non-human... Soften your hearts towards the meaner creatures.[268] *John Wesley*

A print by William Hogarth depicting eighteenth-century cruelty to animals (New Room Archives and Library)

The fight against slavery

The social justice issue for which John Wesley is best remembered is his opposition to slavery and the slave trade. Charles fully supported him because in their time in America he had seen its evil impact at first hand:

Part of the display in the Museum at the New Room on Bristol's role in the slave trade

I observed much, and heard more, of the cruelty of masters towards their negroes... The giving a child a slave of its own age to tyrannise over, to beat and abuse out of sport, was, I myself saw, a common practice. Nor is it strange, being thus trained up in cruelty, they should afterwards arrive at so great a perfection in it; that Mr Star... [for example, should] first nail up a negro by the ears, then order him to be whipped in the severest manner, and then have scalding water thrown over him, so that the poor creature could not stir for four months after.[269] *Charles Wesley*

George Whitefield did not argue for slavery's abolition, but instead urged all Americans to stop treating their slaves with such cruelty and barbarity:

As I lately passed through your provinces, I was touched with a fellow feeling of the miseries of the poor negroes... God has a quarrel with you for your cruelty... It is sinful... to use them worse than brutes... Nay, some, as I have been informed by an eye-witness, have been, upon the most trifling provocation, cut with knives, and had forks thrown into their flesh... [or been cruelly whipped]... My blood has almost run cold within me when I have considered how many of your slaves have neither convenient food to eat, nor proper raiment to put on.[270]

George Whitefield

Whitefield took the highly unusual step of preaching to the enslaved and he tried to create a school for African-Americans in America:

Jesus Christ has died for them, as well as for others... For in Jesus Christ there is neither male nor female, bond nor free. [271]

George Whitefield

Legal cases against holding slaves in Britain brought by a lawyer called Granville Sharpe and the writings of an American Quaker called Anthony Benezet about the horrors of the slave trade made John Wesley become an active anti-slavery campaigner from the 1770s onwards:

I can with truth and sincerity declare, that I have found amongst the negroes as great a variety of talents as amongst a like number of whites; and I am bold to assert, that the notion entertained by some, that the blacks are inferior in their capacities, is a vulgar prejudice.[272] *Anthony Benezet*

Anthony Benezet (public domain)

In 1774 John published the first really successful anti-slavery leaflet and it was printed on both sides of the Atlantic:

Part of the display in the Museum at the New Room on John Wesley's role in the anti-slavery movement

Better no trade than trade procured by villainy... Better is honest poverty, than all the riches bought by the tears, and sweat, and blood of our fellow creatures... What, to whip them for every petty offence, till they are all in gore blood? To take that opportunity of rubbing pepper and salt into their raw flesh?

To drop burning sealing-wax upon their skin? To castrate them? To cut off half their foot with an axe? To hang them on gibbets, that they might die by inches with heat and hunger and thirst? To pin them to the ground and then burn them by degrees?... Notwithstanding ten thousand laws, right is right and wrong is wrong. There must still remain an essential difference between justice and injustice, [between] cruelty and mercy... You act the villain to enslave them... Give liberty to whom liberty is due, that is, to every child of man, to every partaker of human nature... Away with all whips, all chains, all compulsion!... Do with everyone else as you would he should do to you.[273]

John Wesley

John then helped publish accounts of the capture and ill-treatment of slaves. A notable example was the account of a Methodist called Silas Todd who had worked as a sailor on a slave ship:

One of our black slaves, through a violent sickness was worn to a mere skeleton, and as he could not eat his allowance, the savage [Captain] Tucker invented a scheme to compel the slave to eat, and laid to his charge that he was sulky: however, the poor creature could not, nor did he eat. Upon this the captain called for his black cabin boy, Robin, to bring him his horsewhip; he did so, and Tucker began lashing the poor sick man till I fairly believe from his neck to his ankles there was nothing to be seen but bloody wounds. The poor creature made no kind of resistance, nor spoke one word... [The captain]... ordered two ammunition pistols well loaded with ball... and with a malicious and violent grin, pointing one of the pistols to him, told him he would kill him...The captain applied the mouth of the pistol to the middle of his forehead, and fired. The man instantly clapped his hands to his head... the blood gushing from his forehead like the tapping a cask… Tucker then… clapped another [pistol] to his ear and fired that also.[274]

Silas Todd

Wesley also subscribed to have published the first ever autobiography of a former slave:

One day, when all our people were gone out to their works as usual, and only I and my dear sister were left to mind the house, two men and a woman got over our walls, and in a moment seized us both, and, without giving us time to cry out, or make resistance, they stopped our mouths, and ran off with us… They put me into a large sack. They also stopped my sister's mouth, and tied her hands; and in this manner we proceeded… [until] my sister and I were then separated… It was in vain that we besought them not to part us; she was torn from me, and immediately carried away… I cried and grieved continually; and for several days I did not eat any thing but what they forced into my mouth. At length, after many days travelling… I was sold… and again sold… [and eventually sold to] a slave ship, which was then riding at anchor, and waiting for its cargo… I was immediately handled and tossed up to see if I were sound by some of the crew; and I was now persuaded that I had gotten into a world of bad spirits, and that they were going to kill me. Their complexions too differing so much from ours, their long hair, and the language they spoke, which was very different from any I had ever heard, united to confirm me in this belief… When I looked round the ship… [I saw] a multitude

A possible portrait of Olaudah Equiano (Royal Albert Memorial Museum, Exeter)

of black people of every description chained together, every one of their countenances expressing dejection and sorrow... Quite overpowered with horror and anguish, I fell motionless on the deck and fainted... I was soon put down under the decks, and there I received such a salutation in my nostrils as I had never experienced in my life... The stench of the hold... was so intolerably loathsome... The closeness of the place, and the heat of the climate, added to the number in the ship, which was so crowded that each had scarcely room to turn himself, almost suffocated us... This wretched situation was again aggravated by the galling of the chains... The shrieks of the women, and the groans of the dying, rendered the whole a scene of horror almost inconceivable.[275]   *Olaudah Equiano*

Statue of Boston King in Witnesses to Revolution Gallery (American Revolution Museum in Yorktown)

Two escaped slaves, 'Ancona Robin' Robin John and 'Little Ephraim' Robin John, were given sanctuary at the New Room in Bristol until a court case secured their right to return as freemen to Nigeria. After John Wesley's death the society members in Bristol also welcomed a former slave called Boston King and he was educated at Kingswood School in 1794-96. All these three offered thanks to the Methodists for enabling them to appreciate that it was possible for some white people to treat them as fellow human beings:

We can never thank you enough for your love to us... You know how kind our Bristol friends have been to us... We had a very blessed time. Last night [John] Wesley offered us up in a very solemn manner to God and we humbly hope his prayer will be heard.[276]

Ancona Robin

I have great cause to be thankful that I came to England for I am now fully convinced that many of the white people, instead of being enemies and oppressors of us poor blacks, are our friends, and deliverers from slavery, as far as their ability and circumstances will admit. I have met with the most affectionate treatment from the Methodists of London, Bristol, and other places which I have had an opportunity of visiting. And I must confess, that I did not believe there were upon the face of the earth a people so friendly and humane as I have proved them to be… I pray God to reward them a thousand fold for all the favours they have shown to me in a strange land… In the former part of my life I had suffered greatly from the cruelty and injustice of the whites, which induced me to look upon them, in general, as our enemies… [but] the Lord removed all my prejudices; for which I bless his Name. [277]

Boston King

John encouraged Americans to oppose slavery when they began demanding political liberty and many Methodists in the colonies accepted his guidance on the matter:

Slave-keeping is contrary to the laws of God, man, and nature; and hurtful to society, contrary to the dictates of conscience and pure religion, and doing that which we would not another should do to us and ours.[278]

Resolution of Methodist Conference in Baltimore

In the 1780s John became a particularly active member of the growing group of Christians who were dedicated to ending Britain's involvement in the slave trade. Among these was the former captain of a slave ship, John Newton:

Amazing Grace, how sweet the sound
that saved a wretch like me.
I once was lost but now am found,
was blind, but now I see.[279]

John Newton

*John Newton by W.S. Wright 1786
(Cowper and Newton Museum)*

And Newton's close friend, the poet William Cowper, who wrote a
poem on slavery from a slave's perspective:

Men from England bought and sold me,
paid my price in paltry gold;
but though their hearts have enrolled me,
minds are never to be sold.
Still in thought as free as ever,
'What are England's rights', I ask,
'me from my delights to sever,
me to torture, me to task?'
Fleecy locks and black complexion
cannot forfeit nature's claim:
skins may differ, but affection
dwells in black and white the same…
Slaves of gold, whose sordid dealings
tarnish all your boasted powers,
prove that ye have human feelings
ere ye proudly question ours.[280]

William Cowper

William Cowper (public domain)

In 1787 Thomas Clarkson, a deacon in the Church of England, and William Wilberforce, an M.P. who was very friendly with Charles Wesley, created the Society for the Abolition of the Slave Trade, an organisation designed to lobby Parliament:

Thomas Clarkson by H. Room (St John's College, Cambridge)

We come into the temple of God; we fall prostrate before him; we pray to him, that he will have mercy upon us. But how shall he have mercy upon us, who have had no mercy upon others! We pray to him, again, that he will deliver us from evil. But how shall he deliver us from evil, who are daily invading the right of the injured African, and heaping misery on his head!... I had a direct revelation from God ordering me to devote my life to abolishing the trade.[281]   ***Thomas Clarkson***

John immediately offered his support and helped launch the Society in Bristol by preaching to the City's leaders and organising a public meeting on slavery at the New Room:

Wesley addressing the Mayor and Corporation of Bristol by W.Holt Yates Titcumb 1918 (Bristol Museum and Art Gallery)

I gave notice of my design to preach on… the general topic of slavery. In consequence of this… the [New Room] from end to end was filed with high and low, rich and poor… About the middle of the discourse, while there was on every side attention still as night, a vehement noise arose, none could tell why and shot like lightning through the whole congregation. The terror and confusion was inexpressible. You might have imagined a city taken by storm. The people rushed upon each other with the utmost violence; the benches were broken in pieces… Satan fought lest his kingdom be delivered up.[282]   *John Wesley*

Cowper mocked those who refused to listen because they feared that the abolition of slavery would affect their wealthy lifestyle:

> I own I am shocked at the purchase of slaves
> and fear those who buy them and sell them are knaves;
> what I hear of their hardships, their tortures, and groans,
> is almost enough to drive pity from stones.
> I pity them greatly, but I must be mum,
> for how could we do without sugar and rum?
> especially sugar, so needful we see;
> what, give up our dessert, our coffee and tea? [283]
>
> *William Cowper*

John Wesley's last letter before he died was to encourage the continuation of the anti-slavery movement :

If God be for you, who can be against you? Are all of them stronger than God? O be not weary in well-doing! Go on, in the name of God and in the power of his might, till even American slavery (the vilest that ever saw the sun) shall vanish away before it.[284]   *John Wesley*

John Wesley meeting up with William Wilberforce (Wesley His Own Biographer 1893)

Wilberforce asked the first Methodist Conference that met after Wesley's death to help him with an anti-slave trade petition. The result was 229,426 signatures (this compares to the 122,978 signatures that came from all the other nonconformist groups combined). Wilberforce pursued his campaign until Parliament finally banned the trade in 1807 and then he fought for Britain to abolish slavery altogether – a battle that he eventually won in 1833, three days before his own death. In America the Methodist leadership decided to reject Wesley's anti-slavery position but his views continued to have an influence on the anti-slavery movement, including on the remarkable female preacher and campaigner, Dorothy Ripley, who was brought up as a Methodist although she became a Quaker. She met and criticised Thomas Jefferson for advocating liberty whilst possessing slaves when he was the President of the United States:

The tears I shed and bitterness of spirit which I felt for the

African race and the heathen at large, God only knows… I told him God had made all nations of one blood… Enquiring how many slaves the president had, he informed me that some time since he had three hundred, but the number was decreased. It now appeared a seasonable time to signify how my nature was shocked to hear of the souls and bodies of men being exposed to sale like the brute creation, and I implored his pity and commiseration… [I believe God] is secretly working in me and many others in this land… [and that] in the world to come the wickedness and cruelty of every one shall be brought to light… The African race will then witness against their hard and cruel tormentors… and I tremble for every oppressor! for every one who deals hardly to any of God's creatures.[285]   *Dorothy Ripley*

The continuing influence of John Wesley on social justice issues

Methodists remained relatively small in number in Britain but they constituted such a strong presence for change in their communities that some historians used to argue the movement was a major factor in why Britain was able in the nineteenth century to avoid a political revolution and engage in social and political reform relatively peacefully. Even though that claim is usually no longer upheld, historians still agree that Methodism played a key role in the emergence both of trade unionism and of the Labour party in the nineteenth century. It also challenged the Church of England to instigate changes in its approach to social justice issues and helped create a greater interest in education as a means of self-advancement among the working and middle classes:

Passion and prejudice govern the world… It is our part, by religion and reason combined, to counteract them all we can. [286]

John Wesley

7
THE DEVELOPMENT OF
METHODISM
1748-70

Part of the display on Charles Wesley and his hymn writing in the Museum at the New Room

The return of George Whitefield

In July 1748 George Whitefield arrived back in England after four-year absence. He refused to resume leadership of the Calvinistic Methodists, thus effectively ensuring their decline, especially as they had already lost John Cennick and Howell Harris' health collapsed in the 1750s. Instead Whitefield agreed to become the Countess of Huntingdon's

Earl of Chesterfield (public domain) Chaplain so he could try and influence the aristocracy to support the religious revival. More significantly, he committed himself to undertaking preaching nationwide:

> Mr Whitefield's eloquence is unrivalled – his zeal inexhaustible; and not to admire both would argue a total absence of taste and an insensibility not to be coveted by anyone. [287]
>
> *Philip Dormer Stanhope, Earl of Chesterfield*

Historians have tended to focus on the continued division within Methodism, but this ignores the fact that most people are not interested in theological arguments. The vast majority of those who attended open-air preaching recognised there were differences between what was said by Whitefield and other Calvinist preachers and what

Christopher Hopper (New Room Archives and Library) was said by the Wesleys and some of their lay preachers, but they were happy to listen to either or both. Many of John's lay preachers were very happy to encourage crowds to attend Whitefield's tours because of his talent as a preacher and they stressed the importance of avoiding dispute:

> I do not love contention; I am no disputant; I therefore leave polemical divinity to men of learning, abilities and experience. I can only say... I know God is love. I know it by experience... I love holiness and I pursue it... This I call Bible religion, genuine Christianity; and this religion I call mine.[288]
>
> *Christopher Hopper*

Whitefield's powerful preaching therefore continued to ensure that Wesleyan Methodism received a much-needed boost. In the same way Methodism in Northern Ireland benefitted from the work of John Cennick, although he had become a Moravian. The Moravian Church had a public relations crisis in the early 1750s and that meant it then reduced its role in Ireland largely to just creating a Moravian settlement at Gracehill. As a consequence many of the religious societies created by Cennick not only in Ireland but in Wales and parts of England (notably in Wiltshire) eventually drifted towards Methodism after his death in 1754:

> He lived without contention, humble, plain,
> much good to all he daily strove to gain.
> What can be said enough of this dear man,
> who in the paths of virtue steady ran?
> By night, by day, he'd travel far and near,
> through howling wilderness, void of fear.
> Around the globe he willingly would go
> could he but something for his Master do...
> his life one constant pilgrimage indeed...
> From his freed soul flowed every gospel thought

and his life acted what his tongue had taught…
Grace in his heart and mercy to his tongue,
his lips flowed love, and free salvation sung.[289]

Anonymous contemporary

The Moravian settlement at Gracehill

Wesleyan Methodism's greatest strength, apart from its superior organisation, lay in the powerful hymns that were pouring at the rate of almost one a day from Charles' pen:

Soldiers of Christ arise
and put your armour on,
strong in the strength which God supplies
through his eternal Son.
Strong in the Lord of hosts, and in his mighty power,
who in the strength of Jesus trusts
is more than conqueror.[290]   *Charles Wesley*

Whitefield was happy to let John and Charles Wesley become the undisputed leaders of Methodism:

Let my name be forgotten, let me be trodden under the feet of all men, if Jesus may thereby be glorified. [291]   *George Whitefield*

The marriages of Charles and John

As young men John and Charles had vowed to each other that they would remain single in order to have no family distractions from serving God to the full. This had not proved an easy vow to uphold, especially for John who enjoyed flirting with women. As a young man he had come perilously close to breaking his vow when in America and faced with the charms of the young teenager Sophy Hopkey:

> God let loose my inordinate affection upon me, and the poison thereof drank up my spirit. I was… in the sharpest pain I ever felt. 'To see her no more!' That thought was the piercing of a sword. It was not to be borne – nor shaken off. I was weary of the world, of light, of life… [God] forsook me. I could not pray. Then indeed the snares of death were about me: the pains of hell overtook me.[292]
>
> *John Wesley*

Sarah (Sally) Gwynne by John Russell (Charles Wesley's House)

In 1748 both John and Charles found themselves for the first time seriously in love. Charles' choice was Sally Gwynne, the daughter of a Welsh landowner, who was an early supporter of Methodism:

> In the loving openness of my heart, without premeditation, I asked her 'if she could trust herself with me for life' and with a noble simplicity she readily answered me 'she would'.[293]
>
> *Charles Wesley*

John's choice was Grace Murray, the housekeeper at the Orphan

House in Newcastle and one of the first female preachers:

> I saw the work of God prosper in her hands. She lightened my burden more than can be expressed. She gave spiritual counsel… to the believers in every place… She was to me both a servant and a friend, as well as a fellow-labourer in the gospel. She provided everything I wanted. She told me with all faithfulness and freedom, if she thought anything amiss in my behaviour.[294]
>
> *John Wesley*

John opposed Charles' marriage, thinking that Sally was an inappropriate choice because of her privileged background, and he only gave his final consent the day before the wedding was due to take place on 8 April 1749. Charles subsequently made clear his marriage enhanced his work rather than diminishing it:

> More zeal, more life, more power, I have not felt for some years… so… marriage has been no hindrance. You will hardly believe it sits so light upon me.
>
> *Charles Wesley*

The display on Charles' family in the Museum at the New Room

Charles and Sally were to have a very happy marriage. They had eight children but only two sons (Charles and Samuel) and one daughter (Sally) grew to adulthood. Both the sons were musical prodigies – indeed Samuel was described as 'the English Mozart'. Charles upset many Methodists by encouraging his sons' musical talent rather than forcing them to become preachers. He wrote in defence of the musical education given to his son Charles:

> I always designed my son for a clergyman. Nature has marked him for a musician, which appeared from his earliest infancy. My friends advised me not to cross his inclination. Indeed, I could not if I would. There is no way of hindering his being a musician but cutting off his fingers. As he is particularly fond of church music, I suppose if he lives he will be an organist.[295]
>
> ***Charles Wesley***

Charles Wesley junior
(Charles Wesley's House)

Samuel Wesley
(Charles Wesley's House)

Sally Wesley
(Epworth Rectory)

John was not so fortunate in his domestic life because Charles prevented his marriage to Grace Murray. Charles more or less forced Grace to marry the lay preacher John Bennet on 3 October 1749. Charles wrongly thought Grace was just the latest in a line of infatuations rather than the true object of his brother's affection and he thought the lay preachers would be horrified by John 'pinching' her from Bennet, to whom she had been more or less promised in marriage for a couple of years. Charles had also had to deal with protests against Grace's suitability from a number of the female society members in Newcastle. Accompanying Wesley and other preachers on preaching tours had hopelessly compromised her reputation as far as they were concerned. Charles told Grace:

> The case appears to me you promised John Bennet to marry him… So dishonest an action [as to marry my brother] would destroy both himself and me and the whole work of God… [The revival] was on the very brink of ruin, but the snare is broken and we are delivered… O how humbled, how thankful ought you to be at your almost miraculous deliverance! Had the Lord not restrained you what a scandal had you brought upon the gospel, nay, and you would have left your name as a curse upon God's people.[296] *Charles Wesley*

Charles' action may also have stemmed from his awareness that John was ill-suited to marriage. His brother's determination to give everything to God meant that he was very blinkered when it came to what family life meant. Any wife or child would have to accept that John would never put their needs first. Viewing family life as a potential distraction from serving God to the full made John at times stunningly insensitive. Typical of his attitude was what he wrote to his sister Martha over the death of her children:

> I believe the death of your children is a great instance of the goodness of God towards you. You have often mentioned how much time they took up. Now that time is restored to you and you have nothing to do but serve the Lord… without distraction.[297] *John Wesley*

Charles' prevention of the marriage understandably ruined the brothers' close relationship, especially after Sally Wesley had a miscarriage, which Charles attributed to her being upset by John's treatment of her after his failure to marry Grace:

> Heard that my brother was come. Troubled and burdened, yet went to him. No love or joy or comfort in the meeting. No confidence on either side. He did not want to talk with me… He took my wife into his room… and read her his own account, trying all he could to make a difference between her and me. She could say nothing to his confident assertions, though [they were] the grossest misrepresentations and falsifications of facts. This last act of unkindness wounded me more than all the rest.[298]
>
> *Charles Wesley*

The brothers continued to try and create a religious revival, but they worked largely independently for four years. John travelled the country extensively while Charles largely centred his work in Bristol and London, except for occasional preaching tours. In 1752 Charles began working increasingly with Selina Hastings, the Countess of Huntingdon, and with George Whitefield once he had returned again from America. In this he was supported by the then leading Wesleyan lay preacher, John Jones, who was based in Bristol and who had married Sarah Perrin, the housekeeper at the New Room. John urged Charles to once more accept his leadership:

> Either act in connexion with me, or never pretend to it… I mean take counsel with me once or twice a year as to the places where you will labour... At present you are so far from this that I do not even know when and where you intend to go; so far are you from following any advice of mine – nay, even from asking it…. I may say, without vanity, that I am a better judge… [in assessing

where you should preach] than either Lady Huntingdon, Sally, Jones, or any other, nay than your own heart. [299]   *John Wesley*

Whitefield urged Charles not to break entirely with his brother:

The connection between you and your brother, hath been so close and continued, and your attachment to him so necessary to keep up his interest, that I would not willingly for the world do or say anything that may separate such friends. I cannot but help think that he is still jealous of me and my proceedings; but, thank God, I am quite easy about it... I have a disinterested view to promote the common salvation only... [God] knows how I love and honour you, and your brother, and how often I have preferred your interest to my own. This, by the grace of God, I shall continue to do.[300]   *George Whitefield*

George Whitefield by John Russell (National Portrait Gallery)

The brothers' relationship was made worse because John, on the rebound from his failure to marry Grace Murray, married a most unsuitable wife called Molly Vazeille. He thought her an appropriate choice because she had money (and so would incur the movement in no expense) and was too old to have children. Molly proved possessively jealous and ended up abusing John both verbally and physically:

Once, when I was in the north of Ireland, I went into a room, and found Mrs. Wesley foaming with fury. Her husband was on the floor, where she had been trailing him by the hair of his head; and she herself was still holding in her hand venerable locks which she had plucked up by the roots. I felt as though I could have knocked the soul out of her.[301]   *John Hampson*

*Mary (Molly) Vazeille
(Methodist Church Archives)*

They were to eventually separate. Years later John wrote in a final letter to Molly:

You have laid innumerable stumbling blocks in the way of both the wise and unwise. You have… increased the number of rebels, deists, and atheists; and weakened the hands of those that love and fear God. If you were to live a thousand years twice told, you could not undo the mischief which you have done… I bid you Farewell.'[302]   *John Wesley*

It was only when John almost died in December 1753 that the brothers were reconciled, and even then their relationship was never as cordial as it had been. Matters were not helped by their differing response to the wish of some preachers in the mid 1750s to be able to offer Holy Communion. John did not take a strong stand against this but Charles was bitterly opposed, saying the lay preachers had no authority to do so and that it would lead to Methodism separating from the Church of England. Charles won the argument at the 1755 Methodist Conference, but the issue was to keep resurfacing over the coming years:

I have delivered my own soul in this society, exhorting them to continue steadfast in fellowship with the Church of England. The same exhortation I hope to have with every society throughout the land.   *Charles Wesley*

The importance of hymn-singing

John Valton (New Room Archives and Library)

Despite the internal tensions, Methodism continued to expand. A factor in that expansion was the growing practice of encouraging society members to listen to personal testimonies and to reports of what was happening elsewhere:

Under such testimonies I catch a flame from the celestial altar, which glows with hallowing influence. What, shall one member be blessed, and all the others not rejoice? [303]

John Valton

Thomas Tennant (New Room Archives and Library)

But the biggest single contributor to Methodist success was its hymn singing. It was literally a movement 'born in song':

The song of the Methodists is the most beautiful I ever heard. Their fine psalms have exceedingly beautiful melodies... They sing in a proper way, with devotion, serene mind and charm. It added not a little to the harmonious charm of the song that some lines were sung only by the women, and afterwards the whole congregation joined in the chorus.[304]

Johan Hendrik Liden

When I came to the door and heard them singing, I had such an idea both of their goodness and of my own unworthiness, that I durst not [at first] presume to go in.[305]   *Thomas Tennant*

The sound of their singing sometimes even won over their opponents:

Duncan Wright (New Room Archives and Library)

The rabble... contrived that one of them should get into the barn before the people [belonging to the Methodist society] came... [so he could] let his companions in at the appropriate time. To conceal himself the better, he got into a sack and lay down behind the door. When the society were all in, they fastened the door as usual. Soon after came the mob, hallooing and shouting to their friend to let them in... but, being charmed with the first hymn, he thought it a thousand pities (as he afterwards said) to disturb them while singing it... [He was helped out of the sack] bawling and screaming... confessing his sins and crying for mercy. [306]   *Duncan Wright*

Charles' hymns displayed his amazing Biblical knowledge and his strong grasp of theological issues, but they were always Christ-centred:

> O for a thousand tongues to sing
> my great Redeemer's praise,
> the glories of my God and King,
> the triumphs of His grace!
> Jesus! the name that charms our fears,
> that bids our sorrows cease;
> 'tis music in the sinner's ears,

'tis life, and health, and peace.[307] *Charles Wesley*

And rooted in a personal experience that resonated with others:

What we have felt and seen,
with confidence we tell…
We by his Spirit prove
and know the things of God,
the things which freely of his love
he hath on us bestowed. [308] *Charles Wesley*

Charles constantly proclaimed that the grace he had experienced in his own life was equally available to all:

O that the world might taste and see
the riches of His grace!
The arms of love that compass me
would all mankind embrace.[309]

Charles Wesley

Charles Wesley's House in Bristol where a number of his hymns were written

---

John Wesley laid down guidelines on what he expected of those using the hymns written by Charles and others:

1. Learn these tunes before you learn any others; afterwards learn as many as you please.
2. Sing them exactly as they are printed here, without altering or mending them at all; and if you have learned to sing them

otherwise, unlearn it as soon as you can.

3. Sing all. See that you join with the congregation as frequently as you can. Let not a slight degree of weakness or weariness hinder you. If it is a cross to you, take it up, and you will find it a blessing.

4. Sing lustily and with a good courage. Beware of singing as if you were half dead, or half asleep; but lift up your voice with strength. Be no more afraid of your voice now, nor more ashamed of its being heard, than when you sung the songs of Satan.

5. Sing modestly. Do not bawl, so as to be heard above or distinct from the rest of the congregation, that you may not destroy the harmony; but strive to unite your voices together, so as to make one clear melodious sound.

6. Sing in time. Whatever time is sung be sure to keep with it. Do not run before nor stay behind it; but attend close to the leading voices, and move therewith as exactly as you can; and take care not to sing too slow. This drawling way naturally steals on all who are lazy; and it is high time to drive it out from us, and sing all our tunes just as quick as we did at first.

7. Above all sing spiritually. Have an eye to God in every word you sing. Aim at pleasing him more than yourself, or any other creature. In order to do this attend strictly to the sense of what you sing, and see that your heart is not carried away with the sound, but offered to God continually; so shall your singing be such as the Lord will approve here, and reward you when he cometh in the clouds of heaven.[310]*John Wesley*

From the perspective of the Wesleys hymns offered a way of encouraging faith in two ways. First, they were a corporate act that united Christians together and enabled them to worship God in a uniquely heartfelt way:

> Meet and right it is to sing
> in every time and place,
> glory to our heavenly King,
> the God of truth and grace:...
> Vying with that happy choir,
> who chant your praise above,
> we on eagles' wings aspire,
> the wings of faith and love.[311]   *Charles Wesley*

Secondly, they also acted as a source for individual meditation and reflection. Through studying the words of the hymns the early Methodists learned both their theology and what was expected of them in turns of lifestyle:

> In what other publication... have you so distinct and full an account of scriptural Christianity? such a declaration of the heights and depths of religion, speculative and practical? so strong cautions against the most plausible errors; particularly those that are now most prevalent? and so clear directions for making your calling and election sure; for perfecting holiness in the fear of God? [312]   *John Wesley*

Some of the hymn books in the New Room Archives and Library

The many hymnbooks published by the Wesleys, largely a product of Charles' prolific production of over 7,000 of them, was to culminate in 1780 in John's selection of what he judged to be the best 560 hymns written by his brother and others: 'A Collection of Hymns for the People Called Methodists':

> [The] hymn-book you have now before you… is not so large as to be either cumbersome or expensive; and it is large enough to contain such a variety of hymns, as will not soon be worn threadbare. It is large enough to contain all the important truths of our most holy religion, whether speculative or practical; yea, to illustrate them all, and to prove them both by Scripture and reason: and this is done in a regular order. The hymns are not carelessly jumbled together, but carefully ranged under proper heads, according to the experience of real Christians. So that this book is, in effect, a little book of experimental and practical divinity. [313]
>
> *John Wesley*

Part of the display on Charles' role in the history of hymnwriting in Charles Wesley's House in Bristol

The growing revival in Britain and America

John and Charles continued to work largely independently but, as the price for continuing to work within Methodism, Charles forced

John to sign an agreement with four key lay preachers that the Methodists would never leave the Church of England and become a separate Church:

> I stay not so much to to do good as to prevent evil. I stand in the way of my brother's violent counsellors, the object both of their fear and hate... All I can desire of him... [is] to cut off all their hopes of his ever leaving the Church of England... [and] to put a stop to any more new preachers, till he has entirely regulated, disciplined and secured the old ones.[314]   *Charles Wesley*

Whitefield left for another trip to America in 1754 but returned in May 1755. Once again his preaching benefited the Wesleyan societies considerably and, whilst upholding the benefits of belonging to a Methodist society, he also spoke out against creating a separate Church:

> I rejoiced to hear of the great good Mr Whitefield has done in our societies. He preached as universally as my brother... He beat down the separating spirit, highly commended the prayers and services of our Church, charged our people to meet their bands and classes constantly, and never to leave the Methodists or God would leave them.[315]   *Charles Wesley*

He was particularly effective in Scotland where his Calvinist views matched those of most Scots:

> Thousands and thousands, among whom were a great many of the best rank, daily attended on the word preached, and the longer I stayed, the more the congregations and divine influence increased.[316]   *George Whitefield*

At the same time Selina Hastings, Countess of Huntingdon, attracted a small group of clergy and nobility to more openly support the revival, earning herself the title 'the Queen of the Methodists':

> Uphold this star in thy right hand,
> crown her endeavours with success;
> among the great ones may she stand,
> a witness of thy righteousness! [317]   *George Whitefield*

The display in the Museum at the New Room on fourteen different types of published works produced by John. These turned Bristol into the second biggest publishing centre in the country

Nevertheless, John Wesley was increasingly seen as the main leader of Methodism because of his organisational skills, massive written output, and incessant itinerant travelling in which he attempted to visit every society at least once and preferably twice a year:

> The congregations were exceeding large, and the people hungering and thirsting after righteousness; and every day afforded us fresh instances of persons convinced of sin, or converted to God.[318]   *John Wesley*

> It was of uncommon advantage to me to be among the Methodists at a time when both the preachers and the people loved all our discipline, and practised it. I saw the blessed consequences; for few cared to stay among us, but such as retained their fervour for the whole of religion.[319]   *Duncan Wright*

By the late 1750s John Wesley and Whitefield were still preaching extensively across the country, although George's health was rapidly deteriorating following a murderous attack on him in Ireland. Charles had largely abandoned itinerant preaching but was continuing to act as the main leader in the country's two biggest cities, London and Bristol:

> We all agree… that it would be well for us to observe our Lord's saying to his disciples 'Go aside and rest a little'. But the fewness of the labourers has made it hitherto impracticable… We see our calling which is to suffer all things; disrespect and ingratitude in particular from those we serve in the gospel. But we expect no reward till the great Shepherd comes.[320] *Charles Wesley*

Benjamin Ingham was also still a very effective preacher in the north although the crisis in the Moravian Church had led him to leave it. He had eighty 'Inghamite' societies under his direction. His inability to properly organise either them or his lay preachers, plus later internal divisions within his societies, meant that much of his evangelical work was to eventually benefit Methodism after his death in 1772:

> Jesus, my Saviour, full of grace,
> be thou my heart's delight,
> remain my favourite theme always,
> my joy by day and night. [321] *Benjamin Ingham*

All four men were never narrowly sectarian in their witness because they believed true believers could be found in all Christian denominations:

> 'Father Abraham, whom have you in heaven? Any Episcopalians?'

'No!' 'Any Presbyterians?' 'No!' 'Any Independents or Methodists?' 'No, No, No!' 'Whom have you there?' 'We don't know those names here. All who are here are Christians…' Then God help us to forget our party names and to become Christians in deed and truth.[322]

George Whitefield

I do not think either the Church of England or the people called Methodists , or any other particular society under heaven to be 'the true Church of Christ'; for that church is but one, and contains all the true believers on earth… I conceive every society of true believers to be a branch of the one, true Church of God.[323]

John Wesley

Love, like death, hath all destroyed,
rendered all distinctions void;
names, and sects, and parties fall;
thou, O Christ, art all in all.[324]

Charles Wesley

The perfection crisis

In Britain membership within the Wesleyan branch increased from 3,000 to over 8,000 between 1761 and 1763, and its influence was far greater than that because many of those who listened and were affected lacked the time to become formal members. Unfortunately the movement then suffered two setbacks. The first was the loss of both William Grimshaw and George Whitefield in 1763. Grimshaw died after contracting typhus from one of his parishioners and Whitefield opted to return to America again. It had become obvious by then that his preaching days were numbered because of his declining health. Some historians argue that the American colonists might not have sought to create their own country had not Whitefield's repeated visits helped create a sense of 'America'.

Prior to him the colonies had all acted very independently. On this occasion Charles assumed it was unlikely they would ever see the sick Whitefield return:

> My dear brother, I wish you good luck in the name of the Lord, since you are resolved to die in the harness... My wife joins me in cordial love. Remember me. [325]   *Charles Wesley*

The second and far more significant setback arose from what has become known as 'the perfection crisis'. Back in the early 1740s Edward Noyers had caused problems by encouraging people to claim they had become perfect and that problem now re-emerged because of the actions in London of two of the lay preachers, Thomas Maxfield and George Bell. Bell was new to the role but Maxfield was one of the original sons of the gospel. Together they encouraged an increasingly emotional mindset that other preachers found disturbing:

> Mrs Burroughs of Deptford told me, she rejoiced so much when made perfect as to shed many tears, and [she] saw daily... the air full of spirits; the good, resembling stars, or pieces of silver coin, and fewer in number than the evil, which resembled eels or serpents, and entered the mouth, nose and ears of every person, or almost all she met with... I met in band... with Mr Joyce...who has long counted himself perfect. He said Satan brought the figure of a naked woman to tempt him every night; but, on his praying, it disappeared... Mrs Crosby was desired to talk to me on account of her eminence among the perfect... but,

Thomas Walsh (New Room Archives and Library)

being unable to speak of anything above what I knew, she fled from me.[326]

Thomas Walsh

Credulity, Superstition, and Fanaticism by William Hogarth 1762 (New Room Archives and Library)

Reports of the odd behaviour of those claiming perfection began to cause the Methodist movement to fall into disrepute again and many of the other lay preachers could not understand why John did not denounce what was happening:

As the follies and extravagances of... [those claiming to be perfect] I consider them as the devices of Satan to cast a blemish upon a real work of God... Mr Charles hears every week less or more. Why his brother suffers them, we cannot tell. He threatens but cannot find it in his heart to put into execution. The consequence is the talk of all the town and entertainment for all the newspapers.[327]

John Downes

John did not act because, as in his earlier clash with John Cennick, he believed perfection was attainable and he was not prepared to challenge the claims of those who said they had achieved it. To those who argued perfection was impossible, he pointed out the saintly lifestyle of John William Fletcher, a curate in Madeley, who was very supportive of the Methodist movement:

I rejoice likewise not only in the abilities but in the temper of

Mr. Fletcher. He writes as he lives. I cannot say that I know such another clergyman in England or Ireland. He is all fire; but it is the fire of love.[328]   *John Wesley*

Rev. John William Fletcher
(Museum of Methodism)

Fletcher agreed with John Wesley that a person assured of salvation through God's grace was capable of attaining perfect love but he saw the pride of anyone claiming perfection as being a product of indwelling sin:

My perfection is to see my imperfection… I find more and more that it is not an easy thing to be upright before God; many boast of their sincerity and perhaps they may, but as for me I am forced to smite my breast and to say, from all hypocrisy 'Good Lord, deliver me'.[329]   *John William Fletcher*

Some of the leading evangelical clergy like John Newton cut their links with John Wesley and the more conservative clergy once more began asserting their opposition to Methodism, saying it was encouraging religious fanaticism. It was not long before even John had to accept that the behaviour of the perfectionists had become increasingly irrational:

[They are] like a bear garden; full of noise, brawling, cursing, swearing, blasphemy and confusion… Those who prayed were partly the occasion of this, by their horrid screaming, and unscriptural, enthusiastic expression.[330]   *John Wesley*

He was therefore eventually forced to condemn Maxfield and his followers:

> [I dislike] your supposing man may be as perfect as an angel; that he can be absolutely perfect; that he can be infallible, or above being tempted; or that the moment he is pure of heart, he cannot fall from it... [I dislike] your saying a justified person... cannot grow in grace. I dislike your saying that one saved from sin needs nothing more than looking to Jesus; needs not hear or think of anything else; believe, believe, is enough; that he needs no self-examination, no times of private prayer; needs not mind little or outward things... I dislike your speaking of yourselves as though you were the only men who know and taught the Gospel; and as if not only all the clergy, but all the Methodist bodies besides, were in utter darkness. I dislike something that has the appearance of enthusiasm, overvaluing feelings and inward impressions; mistaking the mere work of imagination for the voice of the Spirit; expecting the end without the means; and undervaluing reason, knowledge and wisdom in general... But what I most dislike is your littleness of love... your want of union... your want of meekness, gentleness, long suffering; your impatience of contradiction; your counting every man your enemy that reproves or admonishes you in love; your bigotry and narrowness of spirit, loving in a manner only those that love you... your censoriousness... of all who do not agree with you; in one word, your divisive spirit.[331]
>
> *John Wesley*

John's opposition came too late because George Bell announced that he knew the world was ending on 28 February 1763. This created such panic in London that the civic authorities arrested Bell:

> [Methodism] is the most destructive and dangerous system to government and society that ever was established.[332]
>
> *Letter in Lloyd's Evening Post*

In the wake of this the London societies lost a quarter of their membership. The Countess of Huntingdon and many others wanted John to resign as leader and they urged Charles to take over from him. Charles' standing at this time was still very high, especially as he was continuing to produce a succession of dynamic hymnbooks and his preaching could still be truly inspirational:

> His word was with power; and I thought my Saviour was at hand, never being so sensibly affected under a discourse before. In the evening I heard him again at the Foundery, and all seemed to be comforted and affected by his word. [333]   *John Valton*

Charles refused to replace his brother but he saw the damage that had been done to the movement (it was to take 27 years to make up the loss) and he told John he should have taken his advice:

> Sad havoc Satan has made off the flock… I gave warning four years ago of the flood of enthusiasm that has now overflowed us.[334]   *Charles Wesley*

John temporarily lost confidence, not least because he felt he could lay no claim to perfection himself:

> I do not love God. I never did. Therefore I never believed… I am only an honest heathen… one of the God-fearers… I have no direct witness… of anything invisible or external. And yet I dare not preach otherwise than I do, either concerning faith, or love, or justification, or perfection. And yet I find a decrease of zeal for the whole work of God and every part of it… I want all the world to come to what I do not know.[335]   *John Wesley*

In 1773 John asked the gifted John William Fletcher to take

command but Fletcher said he would only take over if he could do so in conjunction with Charles, whom he deeply admired and loved. The strength of his attachment to Charles is evident in the following passage:

> I am so assured of your salvation that I ask for no other place in heaven than the one I might have at your feet. I even question whether Paradise would be Paradise if you were not there to share it with me. The very idea… that we might one day be parted, grieves my heart and fills my eyes with tears. [336]

John William Fletcher

John depicted as the key Methodist figure in a very special nineteenth drawing – the picture is made up entirely of words in very minute script that tell his story. This is on display within the Museum at the New Room

The outside world knew nothing of these discussions and to observers like Johan Liden, a professor from the University of Uppsala who visited London, John was the undisputed leader of Methodism:

> [John Wesley is] called the spiritual Father of the Methodists… He preached today at the forenoon service in the Methodist Chapel in Spitalfield for an audience of more than 4,000 people… The sermon was short but eminently evangelical. He has not great oratorical gifts, no outward appearance, but he speaks clear and pleasant… He is a small, thin old man, with long and straight hair… [but his]

zeal for the glory of God... is quite extraordinary. His talk is very agreeable, and his mild face and pious manner secure him the love of all right-minded men. He is the personification of piety, and he seems to me as a living representation of the loving Apostle John.[337] *Johan Hendrik Liden*

The death of George Whitefield

George Whitefield was inevitably caught up in the growing tensions between the colonists and the British government, not least because of his great friendship with one of the key American leaders, Benjamin Franklin:

> I am under continued apprehensions... When I consider the warm resentment of a people who think themselves injured and oppressed, and the common insolence of the [British] soldiery, who are taught to consider the people as in rebellion, I cannot but fear the consequences of bringing them together. It seems like setting up a smith's forge in a magazine of gunpowder.[338]
> *Benjamin Franklin*

From America he urged John to support the revival work in the colonies:

> The Gospel range is of such large extent, that I have, as it were, scarce begun to begin... Had my strength permitted, I might have preached to thousands and thousands every day... Here is room for a thousand itinerants. *George Whitefield*

It came as a surprise when Whitefield arrived back in Britain in the summer of 1765. John accepted Charles' negotiation of a formal agreement (the so-called Public Peace Union of 1766) to work more closely with him and the Calvinistic Methodists and to use the chapels which were being created by the Countess of Huntingdon:

'Last night my brother came. This morning we spent two hours together with G. Whitefield. The threefold cord, we trust, will never more be broken… All her chapels … are now put into the hands of us three.'[339]

Charles Wesley

Whitefield saw this as a return to 'the old Methodism' of the early days of the revival and launched himself into major preaching tours:

I am just come from my field-throne. Thousands and thousands attended… Light and life seemed to fly all around… This is the good methodistical, thirty year old medicine… Every stage, more and more convinces me that old Methodism is the thing – Hallelujah!… Ye Methodists of many years standing, show the young ones, who have not the cross to bear, as we once had, what ancient Methodism was.[340]

George Whitefield

Nevertheless, it was apparent the union would be short-lived because of Whitefield's frail health:

I breakfasted with Mr Whitefield, who seemed to be an old, old man, being fairly worn out in his Master's service, though he has hardly seen fifty years; and yet it pleases God that I, who am now in my sixty-third year, find no disorder, no weakness, no difference from what I was at five and twenty; only that I have fewer teeth and more grey hairs.[341]

John Wesley

Whitefield returned to America in 1769. By this stage the Countess had lost all trust in John Wesley. She decided to ignore Wesleyan Methodism and focus just on building her own chapels (collectively known as the Countess of Huntingdon's Connexion). Whitefield died having given one last final public address on 30 September 1770:

> Mr Whitefield rose, and stood erect… He remained several minutes unable to speak; and then said, 'I will wait for the gracious assistance of God; for he will, I am certain, assist me once more to speak in his name.' He then delivered, perhaps, one of his best sermons. 'I go', he cried, 'I go to a rest prepared; my sun has arisen, and by the aid of Heaven has given light to many. It is now about to set – no, it is about to rise to the zenith of immortal glory. Many may outlive me on earth, but they cannot outlive me in Heaven… I shall soon be in a world where time, age, pain and sorrow are unknown. My body fails, my spirit expands.'[342]   *An eyewitness*

The grave of George Whitefield in Old South Presbyterian Church in Newburyport, Massachusetts

John and Charles both paid tribute to Whitefield's immense contribution:

He has for may years astonished the world with his eloquence and devotion... He spoke with fervency of zeal perhaps unequalled since the days of the Apostles. From the pulpit he was unrivalled... Nor was he less agreeable and instructive in private conversation – happy in a remarkable ease of address, willing to communicate, studious to edify... In spite of a tender constitution, he continued to the last day of his life, preaching with a frequency and fervour that seemed to exceed the natural strength of the most robust... The name of George Whitefield will long be remembered with esteem and veneration... How few have we known of so kind a temper, of such large and flowing affections. Was it not principally by this that the hearts of others were drawn and knit to him? Can anything but love beget love? This shone in his very countenance and continually breathed in his words whether in public or in private.[343]

John Wesley

George Whitefield preaching (public domain)

His one delightful work and steadfast aim
to pluck poor souls as brands out of the flame,
to scatter the good seed on every side,
to spread the knowledge of the Crucified,
from a small spark a mighty fire to raise,
and fill the continent with Jesu's praise…
In his unspotted life with joy we see
the fervours of primeval piety:
a pattern to the flock by Jesus bought,
a living witness of the truths he taught.[344] *Charles Wesley*

8
THE ROLE
OF
THE LAY PREACHERS

The main Preachers' Room, part of the accommodation provided for them in Bristol (now part of the Museum at the New Room)

What was expected

The use of lay preachers was essential to the growth of Methodism:

> Give me one hundred preachers who fear nothing but sin and desire nothing but God, and I care not a straw whether they be clergymen or laymen, such alone will shake the gates of hell and set up the kingdom of heaven upon earth.[345] *John Wesley*

From the outset John laid down rules for how his lay preachers should behave:

1. Be diligent. Never be unemployed a moment. Never be triflingly employed. Never while away time; neither spend any more time at any place than is strictly necessary.
2. Be serious. Let your motto be, 'Holiness to the Lord'. Avoid all lightness, jesting, and foolish talking.
3. Converse sparingly and cautiously with women; particularly, with young women.
4. Take no step toward marriage, without first consulting with your brethren.
5. Believe evil of no one; unless you see it done, take heed how you credit it. Put the best construction on everything. You know the judge is always supposed to be on the prisoner's side.
6. Speak evil of no one; else your word especially would eat as doth a canker. Keep your thoughts within your own breast, till you come to the person concerned.
7. Tell every one what you think wrong in him, and that plainly, as soon as may be; else it will fester in your heart…
8. Do not affect the gentleman. You have no more to do with this character than with that of a dancing-master. A preacher

of the gospel is the servant of all.

9. Be ashamed of nothing but sin: not of fetching wood (if time permit) or drawing water; not of cleaning your own shoes, or your neighbour's.

10. Be punctual. Do everything exactly at the time. And in general, do not mend our Rules, but keep them…

11. You have nothing to do but to save souls. Therefore spend and be spent in this work. And go always, not only to those that want you, but to those that want you most…

12. Act in all things, not according to your own will, but as a son in the Gospel. As such, it is your part to employ your time in the manner which we direct; partly, in preaching and visiting from house to house; partly, in reading, meditation, and prayer. Above all, if you labour with us in our Lord's vineyard, it is needful that you should do that part of the work which we advise, at those times and places which we judge most for his glory.[346]   *Rules for the Helpers*

Their role was not just to preach or spend time talking with Methodist bands, classes, and societies, but to spend time talking with individuals and families in their homes. This included paying special attention to any children:

> After a few loving words spoken to all in the house, take each person singly into another room, where you may deal closely with them, about his sin, and misery, and duty…Hear what the children have learned by heart. Choose some of the weightiest points, and try if they understand them…Lead them into it by other questions… Thus, when you have tried their knowledge, proceed to instruct them yourself, according to their several capacities.[347]   *John Wesley*

From the outset there were two types of preacher: those who preached in their spare time and were therefore 'local' preachers, and those who gave up work and travelled the country preaching as 'itinerants'. Much depended on the personal circumstances of the preacher as to which role they undertook and some moved between the two. John thought people benefitted from hearing different preachers:

> I know were I myself to preach one whole year in one place, I should preach both myself and most of my congregation asleep. Nor can I ever believe it was ever the will of the Lord that any congregation should have one teacher only. We have found by long and constant experience that a frequent change of teachers is best.[348]
>
> *John Wesley*

Graffiti scrawled on a pane of glass by three of the many preachers who were assigned to the Bristol circuit (now to be seen within the Museum at the New Room)

Becoming a lay preacher

Most men became preachers in gratitude for what God had done for them:

In that moment it seemed to me as though a new creation had taken place. My soul was filled with light and love. I was now convinced it was my duty to do all I could for God.[349]   *Peter Jaco*

Peter Jaco (New Room Archives and Library)

The whole tenor of my life and conversation was new. Free grace, infinite mercy, boundless love made the change. My heart, my tongue, my hands, were now, in my little way, employed for my loving God. I was no longer of the world; therefore the world began immediately to hate me... [or] pitied me... I thirsted after their salvation, and thought it my duty to promote it... I preached every evening at seven, and every morning at five o'clock, and often at noonday, the common work of a Methodist preacher. [350]

Christopher Hopper

Usually they did not set out to preach but simply began talking to family and friends. Sometimes this was a source of embarrassment to some members of their family:

They begged I would not tell anyone my sins were forgiven; for no one would believe me, and they should be ashamed to show their faces in the street... My wife told me she was ashamed to put her head out of doors for everyone was talking about me, and upbraiding her with my sayings; and she wished I had stayed in London for she could not live with me if I went on as

I did... I answered that I did not care what all the people could say... Then she cried and said that I did not love her so well as I used to do. I replied, 'Yes, I love thee better than I ever did in my life... but if thou wilt seek for redemption in the blood of Christ, we shall be ten times happier than ever'... In a little time all I said was noised abroad and people of all denominations came to dispute with me. As soon as I came home from work my house was filled with people... By these discourses many were pricked to the heart. [351]   *John Nelson*

Occasionally a person first began preaching because a preacher did not turn up and friends encouraged someone to stand in:

The people were waiting... They came to me and asked where he was and what must be done... I stepped to the place, gave out a hymn, prayed, and took those words for my text, 'If ye be risen with Christ, seek those things which are above'... God was pleased to visit us... I preached again at noon, and... in the evening. This... was my beginning, and what I looked upon as my call to preach.[352]   *Thomas Hanby*

Thomas Hanby (New Room Archives and Library)

All recognised it was a big step to take and were usually apprehensive and nervous at first:

I felt a great desire to tell others what God had done for my soul. I wanted my fellow creatures to turn to the Lord, but saw myself utterly unfit to speak... I saw the neighbourhood in which I lived

Thomas Mitchell (New Room Archives and Library)

abounding with all manner of wickedness, and no man caring... [so] I began to reprove sin wherever I was, though many hated me for doing so... After many reasonings in my mind, I ventured to give notice... [that I would preach at a public meeting]. When the time came... my bones shaked and one knee smote against the other... Most of my friends were against me... I made it a matter of continual prayer that... [the Lord] would make my way plain before me.[353] *Thomas Mitchell*

Until John and Charles married there was pressure for any preacher who was unmarried to stay single. This was to avoid the distractions caused by family life, but it was also the case that the itinerant lay preachers were not well-placed to look after a family. They were constantly travelling and they had no fixed income, being entirely reliant on the generosity of the people they visited (it was not until after 1770 that John insisted societies should provide an allowance for preachers with families):

> When shepherds are single,
> they're active and nimble,
> and their hearts [are] above.
> But when they're double,
> they meet with much trouble
> and pay for their love.
> Young babies require
> both clothing and fire,
> and their Mama's tea.
> But when you have none,

> you may up and be gone
> and run the good way.[354]   *Alexander Crumlin*

It was the happily married Charles who first promoted the concept of how a wife could enhance her husband's work providing she was understanding and shared his faith:

> One in will, and heart, and mind,
> each for each by heaven designed,
> one with perfect harmony,
> spiritually one in Thee. [355]   *Charles Wesley*

Nevertheless, it took a special woman to cope with a husband who was involved in itinerant preaching:

> I fixed on the following properties [that a wife should have]… The first was grace… The second that she ought to have tolerably good common sense. A Methodist preacher, who travels into all parts, and sees such a variety of company, I believed ought not to take a fool with him. Thirdly, as I knew the natural warmth of my own temper, I concluded that a wise and gracious God would not choose a companion for me who would throw oil, but rather water, on the fire. Fourthly I judged that as I was connected with poor people, whoever I married should have a small competency to prevent my making the Gospel chargeable to any. [356]   *Thomas Olivers*

From the outset the use of lay preachers was controversial. Most clergy condemned their use. At first the main charge levied against the preachers was that they were secret agents encouraging political sedition, but, when that accusation had to be dropped for lack of evidence, it became common to allege that the lay preachers were frauds, who were motivated by a desire for personal gain:

Thomas Chatterton (public domain)

... straight to Wesley he repairs,
and puts on grave and solemn airs...
The preacher then instructions gave
how he in this world should behave;
he hears, assents, and gives a nod,
says every word's the word of God,
then lifting his dissembling eyes,
'How blessed is the sect!' he cries...
With looks demure and cringing bows
about his business straight he goes.
His outward acts were grave and prim,
the methodist appear'd in him.
But, be his outward what it will,
his heart was an apostate's still.
He'd oft profess an hallow'd flame,
and every where preach'd Wesley's name;
he was a preacher, and what not,
as long as money could be got.[357]

Thomas Chatterton

Assessing the quality of their preaching

At first John Wesley seems to have relied on seeking reassurance that a person was fit for the role by asking the opinion of people whose judgment he trusted:

He is one of the greatest instances of God's peculiar favour that I know... He is my astonishment. The first time I heard him expound, expecting little from him, I sat over against him, and thought what a power of God must be with him to make me give any attention to him. But before he had gone over one fifth part, any one that had seen me would have thought I had been made of wood or stone so quite immovable I both felt and looked. His power in prayer is quite extraordinary. [358]   *Selina Hastings*

He had the power of God and the Spirit with him. I felt the application of it to my soul… It seemed as though 'twas taken into another region.[359]   *Elizabeth Downs*

As the use of lay preachers developed, John commenced giving a possible candidate a period of probation, usually assigning him to work with experienced preachers. If the candidate proved satisfactory, he was formally appointed at a meeting of the Methodist Conference after giving his personal testimony in response to a set of questions:

Have you faith in Christ? Are you going on to perfection? Do you expect to be perfected in love in this life? Are you groaning after it? Are you resolved to devote yourself wholly to God and his work? Do you know the Methodist doctrine? Have you read the Sermons and the Notes on the New Testament [written and published by John Wesley]? Do you know the Methodist Plan?… Do you know the Rules of the Society? Of the Bands? Do you keep them? Do you take no snuff? tobacco? drams? Do you constantly attend the Church and Sacraments? Have you read the Minutes [of the Conferences] ? Are you willing to conform to them?… Are you determined to employ all your time in the work of God?… Will you meet the Society, the Bands, the select Society, the leaders…? In every place? Will you diligently and earnestly instruct the children and visit from house to house? Will you recommend fasting both by precept and example? [360]

John Wesley

Unfortunately the ever-growing demand for preachers from the increase in societies almost inevitably led John to begin appointing preachers without questioning their suitability:

Thomas Taylor (New Room Archives and Library)

I expected to undergo a close examination with regard to my principles, experience, and abilities; and therefore as I did not in everything agree with Mr Wesley, it was a doubt with me whether I should not be rejected. But, to my surprise, I was not asked one question relative to any of these things; but was appointed.[361]   ***Thomas Taylor***

Some men were accepted who were not suitable:

The door to preaching among us is as wide as our societies so that any ignorant or designing man… may preach without any more ado… And there is no man… though never so unfit… but may find at least some old woman who will abide by it that he is the finest man they have ever heard.[362]   ***Joseph Cownley***

Some were able to preach but lived inappropriate lifestyles. One example of that was James Wheatley, who used his position to seduce many women.

He made himself remarkable by introducing a luscious manner of preaching… at once stimulant and flattering… and he was soon detected in fouler practices. Complaint being made of his infamous licentiousness, the two brothers inquired into it, and obtained complete proof of his guilt… Affidavits of the women whom he had endeavoured to corrupt, were printed and hawked about the streets.[363]   *Robert Southey*

In 1751 Charles undertook a major nationwide survey of all the lay preachers to assess their effectiveness. He found most to be very good but with some notable exceptions:

> Such a preacher I have never heard and hope I never shall again. It was beyond description. I cannot say he preached false doctrine, or true, or any doctrine at all, but pure unmixed nonsense. Not one sentence did he utter that could do the least good to any one soul. Now and then a text of Scripture or a verse quotation was dragged in by the head and shoulders. I could scarce refrain from stopping him... Of this I am infallibly sure, that if he ever had a gift for preaching, he has now totally lost it.[364]
>
> *Charles Wesley*

Nevertheless, John was always to speak positively about his decision to use lay preachers and about their role:

> So great a blessing has from the beginning attended the labours of these itinerants that we have been more and more convinced every year of the more than lawfulness of this proceeding. And the inconveniences, most of which we foresaw from the very first, have been both fewer and smaller than were expected. Rarely two in one year, out of the whole number of preachers, have either separated themselves or been rejected by us. A great majority have all along behaved as becometh the Gospel of Christ, and I am clearly persuaded still desire nothing more than to spend and be spent for their brethren.[365]   *John Wesley*

The challenging nature of the role

All the preachers found they had to develop their preaching skills:

> I was twenty-eight years of age, I was an utter stranger to mankind: hence I imagined that blunt honesty, with innocency, would bear me through anything; but I have since learned that we need the wisdom of the serpent as well as the innocence of the dove in our dealings with men... My conduct had not always a due mixture of calm wisdom; my naive impetuosity often hurrying me beyond the bounds of moderation – a thing too common with well-meaning zealous young men. [366]
>
> *Duncan Wright*

Part of the display on the contribution of the preachers and circuits in the Museum at the New Room

Many accompanied John or Charles Wesley or another preacher for a time and copied what they saw of their approach to preaching:

> I had paid a very particular attention to the manner of Mr Wesley, as also of Mr Maxfield, when [they were] preaching in London. I took notice of the pointed and close applications they made to the consciences of the people. As I had them for my pattern I endeavoured to tread in their steps.[367]
>
> *Thomas Rankin*

Some lay preachers were highly educated but most were not and this led even some supporters to question their ability:

I am clearly convinced the want of study ruins half our preachers. Perhaps one reason of their unwillingness to improve themselves may arise from a misunderstanding… [that the Holy Spirit] teaches you all things. True, but not without the use of all other helps… 'Tis the grossest enthusiasm to think to attain the end without the means. Whoever thus vainly dreams, is fitter for a place in Bedlam then to be a preacher of the Gospel. Without making use of every improvement a man is no way qualified for the ministry… The want of this makes their discourses so jejune, trite and sapless; the same dull round notwithstanding the many different texts they speak from… [Mr Wesley] is highly to blame… [for having taken] so many raw, young fellows from their trades to a work they are… utterly unqualified for… One great fault in their preaching is allegorising so much. They find wonders where never… any were placed. The plain meaning of scripture is cast aside, and their whims substituted in room of it.'[368]   *James Norton*

This explains why John Wesley tried to develop Kingswood School as a training base for them and why he spent so much time encouraging lay preachers to study. He not only created libraries in all three of the main centres of Methodism, but personally edited a fifty volume 'Christian Library' that contained extracts and condensed versions of helpful religious books:

Sleep not more than you need and talk not more than you need… Read the most useful books, and that regularly and constantly. Steadily spend all the morning in this employ, or at least five hours in twenty-four… [It is no good to say] 'I have no taste for

reading'. Contract a taste for it by use, or return to your trade…
I will give each of you, as fast as you will read them, books to
the value of five pounds… and I desire all the large societies [to]
provide the 'Christian Library' for the use of preachers. [369]

John Wesley

The demands on those who just undertook preaching in their local
area whilst continuing their normal employment were great:

I had no time for preaching but what
I took from my sleep so that I had
frequently not eight hours sleep in a
week. This, with hard labour, constant
abstemiousness, and frequent fasting,
brought me so low that I was hardly
able to follow my business. My master
was often afraid I should kill myself, and
perhaps his fears were not groundless.
I have frequently put off my shirts as wet

*Alexander Mather (New
Room Archives and Library)*

with sweat as if they had been dipped in water. After hastening
to finish my business abroad, I have come home all in a sweat
in the evening, changed my clothes, and ran to preach in
one or another chapel, then walked or ran back, changed my
clothes, and gone back to work at ten, wrought hard all night,
and preached at five the next morning. I ran back to draw the
bread at a quarter or half an hour past six; wrought hard in the
bakehouse till eight; then hurried about with the bread till the
afternoon, and perhaps at night set out again. [370]

Alexander Mather

The challenges facing the itinerants were of a different nature. They
had to go wherever John Wesley wanted them to go. The country

was divided up into 'circuits' and he usually moved preachers to a new 'circuit' every year or two:

[For 21 years] I have always gone where I was appointed without the least objection... [and] the Lord has made me an instrument in his hand in every circuit where I have laboured for the conviction and conversion of souls. [371]   *William Ashman*

William Ashman (New
Room Archives and Library)

In a country that had few good roads and in which strangers were usually viewed with suspicion, itineracy was both exhausting and demanding:

It is now nine weeks since I began to go round South and North Wales, and this week I came home. I have visited in that time thirteen counties, and travelled most of 150 miles every week, and discoursed twice every day – sometimes three or four times a day. In this last journey I have not taken off my clothes for seven nights, travelling from one morning to the next evening without any rest above 100 miles, discoursing at midnight, or very early, on the mountains in order to avoid persecution.[372]

Howell Harris

Often they faced terrible weather conditions as they travelled, but they were borne up by their faith:

I well remember once on the top of a cold mountain in a violent storm of snow, when the congealed flakes covered me with a white mantle, Satan assaulted me and pushed me hard to return to my school or some other business… I almost yielded to the tempter. But… the Lord… [spoke and] all my doubts and fears vanished away, and I went on my way rejoicing.[373]

Christopher Hopper

Snow – just one of the many hazards (Wesley His Own Biographer 1893)

Many had accidents because of the difficult terrain they crossed and some occasionally faced freak incidents:

Richard Rodda (New Room Archives and Library)

I was one day standing [to preach] on what we call in Cornwall 'a borough of attle' [mining rubble], which filled an old tin pit… While I was standing on its top, it sunk in an instant under my feet; and I literally went down quick into the pit. The attle immediately followed me and covered my head; but I went down till I came where a miner was working, who was greatly surprised to see me. If I had been retarded in my passage, I must have inevitably suffocated. Glory be to God, I received no damage![374]

Richard Rodda

John Jane preaching in the stocks (Wesley His Own Biographer 1893)

The preachers tried to make the most of whatever misfortune befell them:

The first that preached here [in Colne] was John Jane, who was innocently riding through the town when the zealous mob pulled him off his horse and put him in the stocks. He seized the opportunity, and vehemently exhorted them 'to flee from the wrath to come'. *John Wesley*

What made them persevere was feeling that they could rely on God for support:

Jesus was with me in all I did. He gave me light, love, help, joy, peace, and strength in all.[375] *Thomas Walsh*

And a deep sense of the significance of their role:

I saw that the saving of one soul would be of more consequence than anything else under the sun.[376] *Robert Roberts*

Robert Roberts (New Room Archives and Library)

Facing persecution

All the early preachers (and those who listened to them) faced considerable persecution. Sometimes this came from an angry individual:

> She was full of wrath, implacable, unmerciful [against the preacher]… She swore she would have his life, though she was hanged for him afterwards… During the struggle she cut him in three places of his head with a stone so that the blood trickled down… Her husband then stepped in and held her fast in his arms so that she could do no farther mischief…She punched his legs with her feet so that… the blood ran down his legs, she likewise bit several pieces out of his arm and struck the man upon the face with her elbows that the blood trickled down his nose. [377]
>
> *John Bennet*

Mostly the persecution came from mobs gathered together by a few ringleaders:

> They soon got round me and thrust at me… with their poles and staves, but, being kept from striking me by those who held up their hands and arms and took the blows, they proceeded in another way… They rushed at once on one side violently and the form on which I stood then was thrown down… I was scarce down but I was up again, and firmer than before… I could see the men beating and knocking down with their clubs all who kept their ground without any provocation…They seemed to have no regard to age or sex! Both men and women they beat alike… One ancient woman who was, I believe, near fourscore, they knocked down twice. Another woman was so bruised she had to be carried away by horse, which also they beat till it threw

her and the man before her... Others had the blood streaming down their faces... [and many women] they dragged away by their hair, and having thrown them down, trampled on them. [378]

John Cennick

As soon as I began to preach, a man came straightforward and presented a gun to my face, swearing that he would blow my brains out if I spake another word. However, I continued speaking, and he continued swearing, sometimes putting the muzzle of the gun to my mouth, sometimes against my ear. While we were singing the last hymn, he got behind me, fired the gun, and burned off part of my hair. [379] *John Furz*

John Furz (New Room Archives and Library)

They threw me into a pool of standing water. It took me up to the neck. Several times I strove to get out, but they pitched me in again... seven times... Then they let me out... [and] a man stood ready with a pot full of white paint. He painted me all over from head to foot... Then they carried me to a great pond. which was railed in on every side, being ten or twelve feet deep. Here four men took me by the legs and arms, and swung me backwards and forwards... two or three times, and then threw me as far as they could into the water. The fall and the water soon took away my senses... but some of them were not willing to have me drowned... and catching hold of my clothes with a long pole, made shift to drag me out. I lay senseless for some time. When I came to myself... some] swore they would take away one of my limbs if I would not promise to come there no more.[380]

Thomas Mitchell

I did not much regard a little dirt, a few rotten eggs, the sound of a cow's horn, the noise of beers, or a few snowballs in their season; but sometimes I was saluted with blows, stones, brickbats and bludgeons. These I did not well like: they were not pleasing to flesh and blood. [381]   *Christopher Hopper*

Hired mobs trying to prevent preaching (Wesley His Own Biographer 1893)

A few preachers were 'removed' by conscripting them into the army, the most famous being the pacifist John Nelson who refused to fight and turned his subsequent military imprisonment into an evangelical opportunity to convert his jailers and fellow soldiers:

Christianity is a crime which the world can never forgive... [I told them] 'Why do you gird me with these warlike habiliments? For I am a man averse to war, and shall not fight but under the Prince of Peace'... My Master... gives strength according to the day. For, when I came into the dungeon, that stunk worse than a hog-sty by reason of the blood and filth which sink from the butchers who kill over it, my soul was filled with the love of God that it was a paradise to me... And I fell down on my knees and gave God thanks that He counted me worthy to be put in a dungeon for the truth's sake; and prayed that my enemies might be saved from the wrath to come… I wished they were as happy in their own houses as I was in the dungeon… It came into my mind that I had freely received, and I ought to freely give. I therefore preached to them.[382]   *John Nelson*

John Wesley with John Nelson (Wesley Hs Own Biographer 1893)

Those preachers who were engaged in warfare found it hard to witness soldiers whom they had converted dying on the battlefield:

They showed such courage and boldness in the fight as made the officers as well as soldiers amazed. When wounded, some cried out, 'I am going to my Beloved'. Others 'Come, Lord Jesus, come quickly'… John Evans, having both his legs taken off by a cannon-ball, was laid across a cannon to die, where, as long as he could speak, he was praising God and blessing him with joyful lips.[383]

John Haime

John Haime (New Room Archives and Library)

Female preachers

From the outset a few women helped the male preachers, usually by addressing their fellow women, and they became in practice if not in name preachers. Among the first in this category were Sarah Perrin, the housekeeper at the New Room in Bristol, and Grace Murray, the housekeeper at the Orphan House in Newcastle :

> O may I learn to speak the truth with boldness, nay I have thought I should be willing to have less divine sweetness if it would please my master to give me in exchange the gift of edifying others... They invited me to come amongst them. I have been with them several times... I earnestly desire I may lay no stumbling block in their way but that the master... may give me words for edification. I begin to find much openness in declaring my state to others when I think it may be of any service... Call it confessing or what you please.[384] *Sarah Perrin*

Grace Murray in old age by unknown artist (Museum of Methodism)

I had full a hundred in classes, whom I met in two separate meetings; and a band for each day of the week. I likewise visited the sick and backsliders... The work of God was my delight, and when I was not employed in it, I seemed out of my element. We had also several societies in the country, which I regularly visited; meeting the women in the day time, and in the evening the whole society. And oh! what pourings out of the Spirit have I seen at these times! It warms my heart now while I relate it. [385]

Grace Murray

For many years John Wesley encouraged the female preachers to disguise what they were doing so as not to offend the Church:

> In public… intermix short exhortations with prayer; but keep as far from what is called preaching as you can: therefore never take a text; never speak in a continued discourse without some break, about four or five minutes. Tell the people, 'We shall have another *prayer meeting* at such a time and place'.[386] *John Wesley*

The female preachers asserted that they too had a calling to preach from God:

> I believe I am called to do all I can for God… I believe I may speak a few words to the people and pray with them… Several object to this… saying 'A woman ought not to teach, nor take authority over the man'… but I do not apprehend… [that text] means she shall not entreat sinners to come to Jesus… I do not believe every woman is called to speak publicly, no more than every man

Mary Bosanquet Fletcher (public domain)

> to be a Methodist preacher. Yet some have an extraordinary call to it, and woe to them if they obey it not… What I see to be my call, I dare not leave undone.[387] *Mary Bosanquet Fletcher*

> Jesus made me his mouth unto the people, and poured the spirit of love, zeal, and wisdom upon me for their instruction.[388] *Sarah Crosby*

In old age John Wesley became more open to publicly accepting that some women had a call to preach and he even began advising them how best to preach:

> Never continue the service above an hour at once, singing,
> preaching, prayer, and all. You are not to judge by your own
> feelings, but by the Word of God. Never scream. Never speak
> above the natural pitch of your voice; it is disgustful to the
> hearers. It gives them pain not pleasure. [389]   *John Wesley*

This endorsement by Wesley was not supported by all Methodists.
The main criticism often came from other women who accused
them of behaving immodestly and alleged they were seeking to have
affairs with the male preachers:

> Some of our sisters began to… make many objections to me. I
> did all I could to remove them. I called frequently upon them,
> and spoke as lovingly as I could. But it did not avail. They were
> still equally displeased and endeavoured to spread the same
> spirit among others… Till now I had received all things, honour
> or dishonour, the good will or ill will of any, as from the hand
> of God. But now I began to think, 'How hard is this?' To use me
> thus? After I have slaved for them for so many years? Well, I will
> get out of it all. I will leave them to themselves. I will suffer this
> no longer.' By this means I was fretted and weakened, and was
> brought to think of what I had before cast far from me. [390]
>
> *Grace Murray*

Female preachers had to be very circumspect and very determined.
Although some male preachers welcomed being accompanied by a
women, others questioned their right to preach:

> I believe there never yet existed any [group] singularly useful
> to the Church of God who have not been opposed by their

fellow creatures… I have suffered from the world in the way of reproach and slander…[but] in the midst of all, God has given me his approving smile and a blessed consciousness that I was acting under his divine sanction and influence… designing only to promote his glory among men and the real good of my fellow creatures. These have been my constant support under powerful temptation, fierce persecution, and severe affliction… [My being a preacher has] in some few instances exceedingly grieved some of my best friends, which has caused me to weep in secret before the Lord. It has sometimes happened that a preacher would not consent for any female to exhort sinners to come to the gospel.[391]

Mary Barritt

In Wesley's day only the male preachers had portraits taken for publication in the 'Arminian Magazine'. This portrait of 'an unknown woman' is therefore on display in the Museum at the New Room as a reminder of the contribution made by women in early Methodism as band leaders, class leaders, visitors, preachers, etc

The more conservative Methodist leaders after Wesley's death declared the Methodist Church would cease using women as preachers and their work was virtually ignored in early histories of Methodism. Only in recent years have historians started to explore their role:

For many years… I preached in the open air and in barns and in wagons. After I was married I was with my husband in the preachers' plan for many years… I am glad some of our preachers see it right to encourage female preaching.[392]

Sarah Mallett

Coping with the role

Many preachers wrote how God told them what to say:

> God was pleased out of the mouth of the weak to ordain strength.[393]
>
> *Richard Rodda*

Most have left no record of what they preached but there are some exceptions. Here are three brief extracts:

> God knows what terrors can oppress a human creature. He has been a man... When he lays his bleeding hand upon the heart and says, 'Peace, be still' all is healed, and the hurt and pain removed. Remember that when you are troubled, and you know what a broken and contrite heart is, for he will not despise it... And be assured he was sent to heal the broken-hearted.[394]
>
> *John Cennick*

> Be not wise in your own conceits, lest being puffed up with pride, ye fall under the condemnation of the wicked one. Blessed are the poor in spirit. Blessed are the humble and meek... Desire to be (and by following the humble Jesus, you really will be) little and mean in your own eyes... Seek in fervent prayer, that wisdom which cometh from above, which is far from being earthly, sensual, devilish.[395]
>
> *John Bennet*

> Are you tempted to think your sins are of so deep and so aggravating a nature that God either cannot or will not forgive them? Look to the freeness of God's love to me... Are you an unclean person? So was I. Are you drunkards? So was I. Are you liars? So was I. Are you idolaters? So was I. Are you Sabbath-breakers? So was I. Are you disobedient, undutiful, and

rebellious? So was I. Are you unjust? So was I. [396]

Edward Godwin

Some preachers were very active in the various disputes that took place, but most were happy to work amicably with those of different views:

> Forbid disputes, dispel our doubts,
> our wide dissension heal;
> to every servant of the Lord
> thy sacred truths reveal…
> Then concord, peace, and holy love
> shall bless our golden days;
> then all the fold in one glad voice
> shall sing our maker's praise! [397]   *John Cennick*

I trust our Dear Lord will help us… behave to each other in love… Let us then not quarrel… [When we] meet in love with simple minds, open to the truth, weighing fully what is said on both sides, and praying much, we shall be brought to see we aim at the same things. [398]   *Howell Harris*

Some preachers only undertook preaching for a short time but others spent their entire lives as lay preachers and were happy to die 'in harnass':

Every round my husband took lately, being doubtful when he took horse whether he should drop by the way, he carried a paper in his pocket, telling who he was and whither he was going. This day five weeks, being exceeding weak, he feared he should not be able to preach, but I said 'My dear, go into the pulpit and the Lord will strengthen thee.' Neither did he speak in vain : many were comforted and several justified… He died in triumph the next day.[399]   *Mrs Oldham*

Most preachers at varying times testified to receiving strength from God to cope with the strain of the constant travelling or with persecution and the other demands placed on them:

When I consider how the providence of God provided for me in my infancy – brought me up to the state of man – preserved me from those steps which brought others to an untimely end – directed my wandering steps to the means of my conversion –cast my lot among His people – called me to preach His word – owned my preaching to the conversion of others – stood by me in many trials – brought me back, so often, from the brink of the grace – healed my manifold backslidings… When I consider all these things, I must say, 'Surely goodness and mercy have followed me all the days of my life; and I hope to dwell in the house of the Lord for ever'. [400]   *Thomas Olivers*

For he renews my strength as the eagle. I live in holy astonishment before my God while he fills my soul with divine power and the simplicity of a little child… The more I witness for God, the more does he witness in my heart.[401]   *Sarah Crosby*

William Hunter (New Room Archives and Library)

I may say, with humility, it was as though I was emptied of all evil, and filled with heaven and God. Thus, under the influence of his power and grace, I rode upon the sky. My soul fed on angel's food, and I truly ate the bread of heaven. [402]   *William Hunter*

222

They were borne up in part by feeling they were making a difference:

> I find it in my heart to spend and be spent for God, in promoting his glory and the salvation of men… I see more and more that where… [the gospel is not preached] little lasting good is done. I know this is not the way of ease, nor the way to popularity. But as I set out without a view to either, so I hope to continue, by the grace of God. [403]
>
> *Alexander Mather*

And partly by looking forward to a life eternal:

> As a child longs for his father, a traveller for the end of his journey, a workman to finish his work, a prisoner for his liberty, an heir for the full possession of his estate, so I can't help longing to go home.[404]
>
> *Howell Harris*

Field preaching (source unknown)

I believe when I depart out of this world I shall go to him in peace; and when my pilgrimage and war is ended, I shall find rest with him upon his throne; and, without tasting death, his angels shall carry me to his bosom, and I shall enter by the gates into the paradise of God, and follow him upon Mount Zion with the church of the first-born and with the spirits of just men made perfect; with whom I will sit down in white raiment in the temple of God, and go out no more.[405]

John Cennick

9
THE CREATION OF A SEPARATE METHODIST CHURCH IN AMERICA AND BRITAIN 1760-94

Francis Asbury leaves for America from Pill near Bristol (on display in the Museum at the New Room)

The early Methodist societies in North America

It is thought the first Methodist society in North America was created in the log cabin of an Irish farmer called Robert Strawbridge after he emigrated to Maryland in 1760. He is also often described as America's first Methodist lay preacher, although he was not appointed by John Wesley. He preached across Maryland, Pennsylvania, Delaware, New Jersey, and Virginia:

Robert Strawbridge (New Room Archives and Library)

[He was a man] of strong muscular frame… lean of flesh with a thin visage, the bones of his face projecting prominently… [and] a great favourite among the children.[406]

Sarah Porter

Two Irish immigrants, Barbara Heck (known as 'the mother of Methodism') and a carpenter called Philip Embury, whom she encouraged to start preaching, set about creating a Methodist society in New York in around 1766:

Barbara Heck and Philip Embury (New Room Archives and Library)

He spoke at first only in his own house. A few were soon

collected together and joined in a little society – chiefly his own countrymen, Irish… They then rented an empty room in the neighbourhood, which was in the most infamous street of the city, adjoining the barracks.[407]   *Thomas Taylor*

Captain Thomas Webb by Lewis Vaslet 1793 (New York Historical Society Museum and Library)

Captain Thomas Webb, a British soldier who had been severely injured fighting in Canada and become a barracks master in New York, took over as the main preacher:

I admire the wisdom of God in still raising up various preachers according to the various tastes of men. The Captain is all life and fire: therefore , although he is not deep or regular, yet many who would not hear a better preacher flock together to hear him. And many are convinced under his preaching; some justified; a few built up in love.[408]   *John Wesley*

In 1768 Webb helped raise the money for a Wesley Chapel to be built in John Street in New York:

The novelty of a man preaching in a scarlet coat soon brought greater numbers to hear… and obliged the little society to look out for a larger house to preach in. They soon found a place that had been built for a rigging house, sixty feet in length and eighteen in breadth… Mr Embury… [became] more lively in preaching… Great numbers of serious people came to hear God's word as for their lives. And their numbers increased so fast that our house for this six weeks past would not contain half of the people… A young man, a sincere Christian and constant hearer… offered ten pounds to buy a lot of ground [to build a larger place]... and we have reason to hope... [we can raise]... two hundred pounds... I believe Mr Webb and Mr Lupton will borrow or advance [the remaining] two hundred [required].[409]

Thomas Taylor

John Street Methodist Chapel in New York (New Room)

Richard Boardman (New Room Archives and Library)

Captain Webb became a major preacher across five of the colonies and particularly encouraged the growth of a Methodist society in Philadelphia. Having become a Methodist while recuperating from his injuries in Bristol, Webb lobbied the Wesleys to send out lay preachers from Britain. Two lay preachers, Richard Boardman and Joseph Pilmore, agreed to go and work in New York and Philadelphia:

[Charles Wesley]... sent for Mr. Boardman and me into his room, where he spoke freely and kindly to us about our... voyage, and the important business in which we had engaged. After giving us much good advice, he sent us forth with his blessing in the name of the Lord. [410]

Joseph Pilmore

Pilmore took over the shell of an existing church and turned it into the first Methodist chapel in Philadelphia – St George's still survives, making it the oldest American Methodist Church in continuous use:

Joseph Pilmore in copy of painting by C. W. Peale 1787 (New Room Archives and Library)

We met to consult about getting a more convenient place to preach in… [The building] we had would not contain half of the people who wished to hear the word and the winter was approaching, so that they could not stand without. Several places were mentioned, and application was made, but to no purpose. Though the ministers in general were pretty quiet, they did not approve of our preaching in their pulpits. In this, I could not blame them, especially as we form a society of our own, distinct from them and their congregations. What we should do, I could not determine: ground to build upon, might have been easily purchased, but we had no money; and besides we wanted the place immediately. At length we came to an agreement to purchase a very large shell of a Church, that was build by the Dutch Presbyterians, and left unfinished for want of money. As the poor people had ruined themselves and families by building it, they were obliged to sell it to pay their creditors. It was put up at public auction, and sold for seven hundred pounds, though it cost more than two thousand!… Thus the Lord provided for us.[411]   *Joseph Pilmore*

The death of Whitefield in 1770 encouraged John and Charles to take responsibility for the small but growing Methodist movement in America:

Our brethren in America call aloud for help. Who are willing to go over and help them?' [412]   *John Wesley*

Two volunteers were chosen: Richard Wright and Francis Asbury. The latter is now regarded as the father of American Methodism:

Part of the display in the Transatlantic Room in the Museum at the New Room. This display includes Captain Webb's original eye-patch. He is buried in the Broadmead Courtyard outside the New Room

On the 7 August 1771 the conference began at Bristol... Before this I had felt for half a year strong intimations in my mind that I should visit America; which I laid before the Lord, being unwilling to do my own will, or to run before I was sent... At the Conference it was proposed that some preachers should go over to the American continent. I spoke my mind, and made an offer myself. It was accepted by Mr Wesley and others, who judged that I had a call... From Bristol I went home to acquaint my parents with my great undertaking, which I opened in as gentle a manner as possible. Though it was grievous to flesh and blood, they consented to let me go... Many of my friends were struck with wonder when they heard of my going... Whither am I going To the New World? What to do? To gain honour? No, if I know my own heart. To get money? No: I am going to live to God, and to bring others so to do... The people God owns in England are the Methodists. The doctrines they preach, and the discipline they enforce, are, I believe, the purest of any people now in the world. The Lord has greatly blessed these doctrines and this discipline in the three kingdoms: they must therefore be pleasing to him.[413]

Francis Asbury

Francis Asbury by W.E. Whitehouse (Museum of Methodism)

Asbury was impressed by the warm welcome he received:

I know the life and power of religion is here... I think the Americans are more ready to receive the word of God than the English.[414]

Francis Asbury

In 1772 he followed in the footsteps of Whitefield and began undertaking massive preaching tours (often travelling forty to fifty miles a day) but he also copied John Wesley's approach in organising the religious societies. He told the growing number of home grown American lay preachers:

'If possible visit from house to house, and that regularly once a fortnight for no other purpose than to speak to each in the family about their souls... Sermons ought to be short and pointed in town, briefly explanatory and then to press the people to conviction, repentance, faith and holiness... So shall we speak not so much by system but by life and application in the heart, little illustration and great fervency in the spark of life. We have cold weather but we may have warm hearts, faith to.... [move] mountains of sin and rivers of ice. [415]   *Francis Asbury*

Memorial statue of Francis Asbury on horseback in Washington D.C. (Mike Maguire: Creative Commons)

When Captain Webb returned to England, he became the advocate for sending more preachers from Britain. In 1772 it was agreed Thomas Rankin and George Shadford would go:

George Shadford (New Room Archives and Library)

I went to the Leeds Conference, where I first saw Captain Webb. When he warmly exhorted preachers to go to America I felt my spirit stirred within me to go; more especially when I understood that many hundreds of precious souls were perishing through lack of knowledge, scattered up and down in various parts of the country, and had none to warn them of their danger. When I considered that we had in England many men of grace and gifts far superior to mine, but few seemed to offer themselves willingly, I saw my call the more clearly. Accordingly Mr. Rankin and I offered ourselves to go the spring following.[416]   *George Shadford*

From then on John Wesley was totally committed to assisting the work in America:

I let you loose... on the great continent of America. Publish your message in the open face of the sun, and do all the good you can.[417]   *John Wesley*

The American War of Independence

John Wesley engaged in the national debate over the American colonists desire for greater freedom and independence. He and Charles felt they had some genuine grievances:

I am of neither side, and yet of both... We love all, and pray for all, with a sincere and impartial love. Faults there may be on both sides.[418]   ***Charles Wesley***

John asked all the American preachers to promote peace and not war:

My dear brethren, you were never in your lives in so critical a situation as you are at this time. It is your part to be peacemakers; to be loving and tender to all; but to addict yourselves to no party. In spite of all solicitations, of rough or smooth words, say not one word against one side or the other side... Do all you can to help and soften all.[419]   *John Wesley*

The brothers gave support to the colonists until they went to war in 1776 to win independence. Then they urged all American Methodists to have nothing to do with the conflict. Both brothers believed in the divine right of kings and saw rebellion as totally unacceptable:

> None takes away their lives, or freedom, or goods; they enjoy them all quiet and undisturbed... What they claim is not liberty; it is independency... [No man has a right] to be independent or governed only by himself... There is most liberty of all, civil and religious, under a limited monarchy; there is usually less under an aristocracy, and least of all under a democracy.[420]

> *John Wesley*

The declaration of American independence painted by John Trumbull 1819 (public domain)

It was from their perspective a war that could have been avoided had the British authorities been more reasonable and a few of the American leaders less hot-headed:

> See! Here are some thousands of our brave countrymen gathered together on this plain; they are followed by the most tender and feeling emotions of wives, children, and an innumerable

multitude of their thoughtful, humane, and sympathising countrymen. Then turn your eyes and see a superior number at a little distance, of their brethren, 'flesh of their flesh and bone of their bone', who only a few years since emigrated to the dreary wilds of America. These are also followed with the most tender feelings of wives, children, and countrymen. See they advance towards each other, well prepared with every instrument of death! But what are they going to do? To shoot each other through the head or heart; to stab and butcher each other, and hasten (it is to be feared) one another into the everlasting burnings. Why so? What harm have they done each other?… How is wisdom perished from the wise! What a flood of folly and madness has broke in upon us![421]   *John Wesley*

Display on John Wesley's views on what constitutes an unjust war in the Museum at the New Room

The war posed many problems for the preachers that Wesley had sent and all but two returned to England:

Early in the morning of August 27th some of our kind friends came and told me that they were informed that a company of militia, with their officers, intended to come and take me and the other preachers up. Some of our good women came, and with tears, would have persuaded me to leave the place and go to some other friend's house for safety. I answered: 'I am come hither by the providence of God; I fear nothing, and will abide the consequences, be what they will.' Soon after I went to the arbour, which was fitted up for preaching, and then I beheld the officers and soldiers in the outskirts of the congregation. I had not spoken ten minutes, when a cry went through all the people, and I observed several of the officers, as well as many of the soldiers, trembling as they stood.

Thomas Rankin (New Room Archives and Library)

I was informed afterwards by some of our friends, that some of the officers said, 'God forbid that we should hurt one hair of the head of such a minister of Christ, who has this day so clearly shown us the way to salvation'. The noise and tumult occasioned by the British army marching through the province threw everything into confusion, and mad it unsafe for me to travel.[422]

Thomas Rankin

Those Methodists in America who refused to fight for independence faced opposition and often persecution:

George Washington (public domain)

Mr Wesley I know; I respect Mr Wesley; but Mr Wesley, I presume, never sent you to America to interfere with political matters. Mr Wesley sent you to America to preach the gospel to the people. Now you go and mind your proper work: preach the gospel and leave politics to me and my brethren.[423]   *George Washington*

The Wesleyan refusal to support the struggle for independence ensured that the political authorities in Britain ceased to view Methodism with suspicion and opened the way for John Wesley to become a more accepted public figure. A symbol of Methodism's greater acceptance was the building of the New Chapel (later known as Wesley's Chapel) in City Road in London to replace the old Foundery. It opened in November 1778 with a purpose-built house next to it for the ageing John to have as his home.

It is perfectly neat, but not fine; and contains far more people than the Foundery... I preached on part of Solomon's prayer at the dedication of the Temple. [424]   *John Wesley*

The City Road Chapel in London (Wesley His Own Biographer 1893)

Because of John's constant travelling, Charles became the main preacher at the Chapel. Since 1771 he had made London his main base, although he had continued to visit Bristol regularly. Charles put his life at risk in 1780 when he opposed the major anti-Catholic riots that swept across London:

> Imagine the terror of the poor papists. I prayed with the preachers at the chapel, and urged them to keep the peace. I preached peace and charity, the one true religion, and prayed earnestly for the trembling persecuted Catholics. Never have I found such love or them as on this occasion. [425] *Charles Wesley*

Newgate prison set on fire as part of the Gordon Riots (public domain)

Steps towards separation from the Church of England

By the time the Americans won their independence there were an estimated 15,000 Methodist members scattered across forty-six circuits in the new country and there were 83 American itinerant lay preachers. The Americans understandably wanted to create a separate Methodist Church and their promotion of the importance of independence inevitably led some Methodists in Britain to question whether they should also free themselves from the constraints of the unwelcoming Church of England. Charles Wesley was left as the main advocate for staying within the Church. For that reason those preachers who wanted to create a separate Methodist Church began lobbying that they should take control of the preaching in the New Chapel in London rather than have Charles as its main pastor.

Charles wrote to John to defend his continued role:

> My reasons for preaching in the New Chapel twice every Sunday
> are (1) because, after you, I have the best right, and (2) because I
> have so short a time to preach anywhere; (3) because I am fully
> persuaded I do more good there than in any other place. They,
> I know, are of a different opinion and make no secret of it...
> The lay preachers affect to believe that I act as a clergyman in
> opposition to them. To me, it seems that I act as I do in goodwill
> to them, as well as to the people... I thank God the chapel is
> well filled. Last Sunday I preached twice, never with greater and
> seldom with equal effect. I think the preachers wrong, and in
> the greatest danger through pride, but I have and will have no
> quarrel with them. Convince them, if you can, that they want a
> clergyman over them to keep them and the flock together... If
> God continues my strength, I shall take best care of the chapel I
> can till your return. Then I shall deliver up the charge to you and
> you alone.[426]
>
> *Charles Wesley*

Unfortunately for Charles the Church of England was refusing to
send out clergy to America and this fuelled the demand for the
creation of a separate Methodist Church in America. John's first
response was to lobby the Bishop of London to change the Church's
approach:

> I mourn for poor America; for the sheep scattered up and down
> therein. Part of them have no shepherds at all, particularly in the
> northern colonies; and the case of the rest is little better.[427]
>
> *John Wesley*

The Bishop refused to listen and showed his hostility to anyone
linked to Methodism by entering into a legal battle with Selina

Hastings, the Countess of Huntingdon, over her creation of chapels, effectively forcing her to register them as nonconformist meeting-houses because they stood outside the parish system:

> I am to be cast out of the Church for what I have been doing these forty years – speaking and living for Jesus Christ. [428]
>
> *Selina Hastings*

Aware that his life was nearing its end, John Wesley produced the 1784 Deed of Declaration which sought to define how Methodism would be run after his death. This controversially handed decision-making over to one hundred selected lay preachers. Charles was convinced that this would lead to disaster and, feeling himself to be old and marginalised, hoped his friend John William Fletcher might take control:

> I trust… [you will] gather up the wreck. Be sure the sheep will be scattered… Many will find shelter among the Moravians. Many will turn to the Calvinists, Baptists, Presbyterians, and Quakers. Most, I hope, will return to the bosom of their mother, the Church of England. Not one but several sects will arise and Methodism will be broken into a 1,000 pieces.[429] *Charles Wesley*

It took all the efforts of Fletcher to ensure that division of opinion did not lead to disunity and infighting at the annual Conference:

> Never, never, while memory holds her seat, shall I forget with what ardour and earnestness Mr. Fletcher expostulated, even on his knees, both with Mr. Wesley and the preachers. To the former he said, 'My father! my father! they have offended, but they are your children.' To the latter he exclaimed, 'My brethren! my brethren! he is your father!' and then, portraying the work

in which they were unitedly engaged, fell again on his knees, and with much fervour and devotion engaged in prayer. The Conference was bathed in tears; many sobbed aloud. [430]

Charles Atmore

The continued refusal of the Church to send out clergy to the United States forced John to accept the creation of a separate 'Methodist Church' in America. In September 1784 he appointed Thomas Coke, a clerical supporter of Methodism, to work with Asbury in creating a separate Church and he 'ordained' two

Thomas Coke based on 1799 drawing by Henry Edridge (public domain)

lay preachers, Richard Whatcoat and Thomas Vasey, to assist him as presbyters:

[In America] those who had been members of the Church had none either too administer the Lord's supper or to baptise their children. They applied to England over and over; but it was to no purpose. Judging this to be a case of real necessity, I… exercised that power which I am fully persuaded the great Shepherd… has given me. I appointed three of our labourers to go and help them, by not only preaching the word of God, but likewise by administering the Lord's supper and baptising their children, throughout that vast tract of land, a thousand miles long and some hundreds broad. These are the steps which, not of choice, but necessity, I have slowly and deliberately taken. If anyone be pleased to call this separating from the Church, he may. [431]

John Wesley

Charles was not told in advance of John's intentions and was horrified:

Richard Whatcoat and Thomas Vasey, the lay preachers ordained by John Wesley

I can scarcely yet believe it, that, in his eighty-second year, my brother, my old, intimate friend and companion, should have assumed the episcopal character... to ordain our lay preachers in America... He never gave me the least hint of his intention. How was he surprised into so rash a action?... Lord Mansfield told me last year that 'ordination was separation'. This my brother does not and will not see, or that he has renounced the principles and practice of his whole life... [and] acted contrary to all his declarations, protestations, and writings... and left an indelible blot on his name.[432]

Charles Wesley

In America at a Conference held at Christmas in 1784 Francis Asbury and Thomas Coke agreed that the Methodist Church of America should have bishops and that they should become the first two. This was against John Wesley's wishes and it further incensed Charles:

The ordination of Asbury and creation of the Methodist Episcopal Church engraved by A.Gilchrist after painting by Thomas Coke Ruckle (New Room Archives and Library)

A Roman emperor 'tis said,
his favourite horse a consul made:
But Coke brings other things to pass,
He makes a bishop of an ass.[433]   *Charles Wesley*

Charles did not cut himself off from his brother but he resigned his leadership role within Methodism:

> There is no danger of our quarrelling, for the second blow makes the quarrel; and you are the last man on earth I would seek to quarrel with... I [have] kept as close to you as close could be : for I was all the time at your elbow... My heart is as your heart. Whom God has joined, let no man put asunder... In the love which never faileth I am your affectionate friend and brother. Our partnership is here dissolved, but not our friendship. I have taken him for better or worse, till death do us part, or rather, re-unite us in love inseparable. [434]   *Charles Wesley*

It did not help the movement that at this critical juncture John William Fletcher died. Both John and Charles Wesley mourned his passing:

> Many exemplary men have I known, holy in heart and life, within fourscore years. But one equal to him I have not known – one so inwardly and outwardly devoted to God. So unblameable a character in every respect I have not found either in Europe or America.[435]   *John Wesley*

John was left to face the increasing demands from British Methodists at subsequent Conferences that they too should form a separate church:

The more I reflect the more I am convinced that the Methodists ought not to leave the Church. I judge that to lose a thousand, yea ten thousand, of our people would be a less evil than this… Our glorying has hitherto been not to be a separate body.[436]

John Wesley

The death of the brothers

Charles grieved deeply over what he saw as the inevitable separation of the Methodists from the Church of England and it probably contributed to his death on 28 March 1788:

> Happy the days when Charles and John
> by nature and by grace were one,
> the same in office as in name,
> their judgements and their will the same…
> In infancy their hopes and fears,
> in youth, and in their riper years,
> their hearts were to each other known,
> attun'd in perfect unison.[437]

Charles Wesley

Last picture of Charles Wesley in Wesleyan Magazine before his death (New Room Archives and Library)

His last hymn was dictated to his wife a few days before he died:

> Jesus, my only hope Thou art,
> strength of my failing flesh and heart.
> O could I catch a smile from Thee
> and drop into eternity![438]

Charles Wesley

Even those who had fought with him over the issue of separation, paid tribute to Charles:

Mr Charles Wesley died just as anyone who knew him might have expected. I have had the pleasure and profit of his acquaintance for years, and shall have a great loss of a true friend now that he is gone. I visited him often in his illness and sat up with him all night, the last but one of his life... He said many things about the cause of God, and the preachers, that did him much credit... His general character was such as at once adorned human nature and the Christian religion. He was candid, without weakness; and firm, without obstinacy. He was free from the indifference of lifeless formality and the fire of enthusiastic wildness. He was never known to say anything in commendation of himself, and never was at a loss for something good to say of his divine Master. His soul was formed for friendship in affliction, and his words and letters were a precious balm to those of a sorrowful spirit. He was courteous without dissimulation, and honest without vulgar roughness. He was a great scholar without ostentation. He was a great Christian without any pompous singularity, and a great divine without the least contempt for the meanest of his brethren.[439]

Samuel Bradburn

Samuel Bradburn (New Room Archives and Library)

His wife later wrote of him:

It has been remarked that public men do not often shine in private life. Though he regarded 'all the world as his parish', and every man as his brother, Charles was amiable in his domestic circle, and kind to his relations, especially to those who were dependent upon him, or whom he thought neglected and oppressed. Charles was full of sensibility and fire; his patience and meekness were neither the effect of temperament or reason, but of divine principles. John affectionately discharged the social duties, but Charles seemed formed by nature to repose in the bosom of his family. Tender, indulgent, kind, as a brother, a husband, a father, and a master; warmly and inalienably devoted to his friend; he was a striking instance that general benevolence did not weaken particular attachments... His most striking excellence was humility; it extended to his talents as well as virtues; he not only acknowledged and pointed out but delighted in the superiority of another, and if ever there was a human being who disliked power, avoided pre-eminence, and shrunk from praise, it was Charles Wesley... His poetical talents... breathed not only the spirit of poetry... [but] the religion of the heart. As a preacher he was impassioned and energetic, and expressed the most important truths with simplicity, brevity, and force. [440]

Sally Wesley

John Wesley supported by Dr Hamilton and Joseph Cole in 1790 (New Room Archives and Library)

Much of John's time at this stage was taken up campaigning against slavery and the slave trade. His commitment to preaching remained undiminished despite his growing frailty:

My bodily infirmities still continue... so that now I can walk but little. Sometimes the loss of memory in the pulpit has obliged me to stop, and I have been ready to fall down. [Yet] under all my weaknesses, the Lord still blesses my word in the conviction and conversion of souls... I have reason to believe that my love of God has increased... I feel more indifferent to the praise or dispraise of men... I feel the same love to souls, and desire to lay out my life to do them good, and advance the Redeemer's kingdom. I have no desire, no notion, of living for anything but to serve the church.[441]   *John Wesley*

John preached his last sermon on 22 February 1791 and died on 2 March. His last words were:

The best of all is God is with us.[442]   *John Wesley*

Death of John Wesley by Marshall Claxton 1842 (Museum of Methodism)

A number of preachers testified to his influence on them:

> I must declare that every hour I spent in his company afforded me fresh reasons for esteem and veneration. So fine an old man I never saw. The happiness of his mind beamed forth in his countenance... Wherever he went, he diffused a portion of his one felicity. Easy and affable in his demeanour, he accommodated himself to every sort of company, and showed how... courtesy may be blended with the most perfect piety. In his conversation, we might be at a loss whether to admire most his fine classical taste, his extensive knowledge of men and things, or his overflowing goodness of heart. While the grave and serious were charmed with his wisdom, his sportive sallies of innocent mirth delighted even the young and thoughtless; and both saw, in his uninterrupted cheerfulness, the excellency of true religion... [All who shared his company] would subscribe to all I have said. For my part, I never was so happy as while with him.[443] *Alexander Knox*

And many other people paid tribute to John, including in the press:

> His indefatigable zeal in the discharge of his duty has long been witnessed by the world... He laboured, and studied, and preached, and wrote to propagate what he believed to be the Gospel of Christ... He allowed himself so little repose that he seemed to be above the infirmities of nature... Had he loved wealth, he might have accumulated it without bounds. Had he been fond of power, his influence would have been worth courting by any party. I do not say he was without ambition; he had that which Christianity need not blush at...The ardour of his spirit was not neither damped by difficulty or subdued by

age... [and his ability to inspire] made his exit resemble an apotheosis rather than a dissolution... I do not say he was without faults or above mistakes, but they were lost in the multitude of his excellencies and virtues... His great object was to revive... the Church of England... yet for this he was treated as a fanatic and an imposter, and exposed to every species of slander and persecution... [But] he lived to see the plant he had reared spreading its branches far and wide... No sect, since the first ages of Christianity, could boast a founder of such extensive talents and endowments... The great purpose of his life was doing good... The souls of all men were equally precious in his sight, and the value of an immortal creature beyond all estimation... He communicated the light of life to those who sat in darkness and the shadow of death.

Apotheosis: John Wesley that excellent minister of the Gospel carried by angels into Abraham's bosom by unknown artist 1791 published R.Sayer, London (New Room Archives and Library)

Contemporary press account

After much internal fighting the Methodists agreed to take steps that effectively separated them from the Church of England in the 1795 Plan of Pacification. In effect this created the Methodist Church of Great Britain as a separate organisation from the Church of England.

10

Prayers Written By John And Charles And By Their Mother, Friends, And Associates

*John and Charles Wesley: the large bas-relief of the brothers
in the Preachers' Room in the Museum at the New Room
(based on the sculpture of them in Westminster Abbey)*

A prayer before prayer

1

Enable me, Lord, to collect and compose my thoughts before approaching you in prayer... Save me from engaging in rash and precipitate prayers and from abruptly ceasing to prayer to follow business or pleasure as though I had never prayed.[444]

Susanna Wesley

Prayers for early morning

2

O Lord God Almighty... I bless your holy name for all your goodness and loving kindness to me... for my creation and preservation, for all the blessings of this life, and... for bringing me safe to the beginning of a new day... Grant that this day I do not fall into sin, nor run into any danger... May I be able to withstand the temptations of the world, the flesh, and the devil with a pure heart and mind... that I may serve you with a quiet mind, and bring forth the fruit of good works... through Jesus Christ, my Saviour and Redeemer. Amen.[445] *John Wesley*

Samuel Johnson meeting John Wesley and one of his sisters (Wesley His Own Biographer 1893)

3

Make me remember, O God, that every day is your gift and ought to be used according to your command... through Jesus Christ our Lord.[446]

Samuel Johnson

4

God of all goodness I praise and bless your name for... bringing me safe to behold the light of a new day. Send down your heavenly grace into my soul that I may be enabled to worship you and serve you as I ought to do... Do not let me hurt anyone by word or deed. Make me just and honest in all I do. Let me not bear any malice or hatred in my heart... through Jesus Christ our Lord. Amen. [447]   *John Wesley*

Prayers for a stronger faith:

5

O my Father, my God, I am in your hand; and may I rejoice above all things in being so. Do with me what seems good in your sight; only let me love you with all my mind, soul and strength... Deliver me, O God, from a slothful mind, from all lukewarmness, and all dejection... Give me a lively, zealous, active and cheerful spirit that I may vigorously perform whatever you command, thankfully suffer whatever you choose for me, and be ardent to obey in all things your holy love. [448]

John Wesley

6

Pardon, good Lord, all my former sins, and make me every day more zealous and diligent... be present always in my mind, and let your love fill and rule my soul, in all those places, and companies, and employments to which you call me this day... Let all Christians live up to the holy religion they profess.[449]

John Wesley

7

O my bleeding, dying, dear exalted Saviour... unlock, unhinge, and open wide my heart, expand and stretch it out that it may receive of thine immensity… let the stream of thy most precious blood circulate through my soul.[450]   *Elizabeth Johnson*

8

Help me, Lord, to remember that religion is not to be confined to the church or closet, nor exercised only in prayer and meditation, but that everywhere I am in your presence. So may my every word have a moral content… and may all things… afford me an opportunity of exercising some virtue and daily learning and growing toward your likeness. Amen.[451]

Susanna Wesley

9

Teach me to adore all your ways, though I cannot comprehend them… Claim me as your right, keep me as your charge, love me as your child! Fight for me when I am assaulted, heal me when I am wounded, and revive me when I am destroyed… Direct my paths and teach me to set you always before me. [452] *John Wesley*

Prayer for forgiveness and renewal:

John Cennick (New Room Library and Archives)

10

Look upon me; behold a poor sinner at your feet who cannot do without you… I cannot rest, nor sleep, nor wake, nor live, nor die in peace till you assure me that you have forgiven me… Have mercy on me… [because] I am weary with sinning… and beg pardon… Teach me to be faithful and true. Cause me to cleave to you and never go

away... Fulfil my desire that I may love you and live to your praise...
[and] glorify your dear and holy name for ever. [453]   *John Cennick*

11

O Jesus, full of grace and truth... open your arms and take me
in... and love me. Restore my fallen spirit... forgive, and bid me
sin no more. Repair the ruins of my soul and make my heart a
house of prayer... that I may never dare to offend you more. [454]

Charles Wesley

Prayers for understanding the Bible

12

Give me grace to study... daily that the more I know you, the
more I may love you. Create in me a zealous obedience to all your
commands, a cheerful patience under all your chastisements,
and a thankful resignation to all your disposals... O let it be the
one business of my life to glorify you, by every thought of my
heart, by every word of my tongue, by every work of my hand. [455]

John Wesley

13

Shine in the darkness... and give me light to guide my
wandering feet aright so I walk in all your ways... Guide me by
your wisdom and in comparison let me see all other knowledge
as being trivial, void and vain. [456]   *Charles Wesley*

Prayers for humility

14

God, give me a deep humility, a well-guided zeal, a burning
love. [457]   *George Whitefield*

George Whitefield (New Room Archives and Library)

15

Lord, that I may learn of you,
give me true simplicity...
let me cast myself aside,
all that feeds my knowing pride;
not to man, but God submit,
lay my reasonings at your feet...
Then, infuse the teaching grace,
Spirit of truth and righteousness;
knowledge, love divine, impart
life eternal to my heart. [458]

Charles Wesley

16

Help me to appreciate that my greatest joy is that Jesus has done so much for me and my greatest grief is that I have done so little for Jesus. [459]

William Grimshaw

Prayers to resist temptation

17

Lord, give me a continual sense of your presence. Then I shall not easily yield to this or any other temptations.[460] *Mary Gilbert*

18

O merciful God... I look upon you as my friend, my only refuge and constant benefactor. When I grieve for my sins, it is not for fear of punishment, but from the cutting reflection of my black ingratitude in offending my creator and preserver, the God in whom I live and move and have my being, the God to whom I owe infinitely more than I can conceive... [Let me] give thanks and say continually 'Lord, not my will, but yours be done.'

Amen[461]   *Mrs Lefevre*

19

Lord, make me more like you in the inward disposition of my heart, then shall my outward conduct be agreeable to your word and will. [462]   *Mary Entwisle*

20

May I be careful to maintain a constant, habitual sense of you in my mind; to live and act in your presence; to think often of your power, wisdom, goodness, justice, truth and, above all, your infinite purity, that it may be a check upon my mind and best preservative against all temptations.[463]   *Susanna Wesley*

Prayer in times of adversity

21

Susanna Wesley (New Room Archives and Library)

Be with me, O God, in a time of deep adversity, which is apt to affect my mind too much and to dispose to anxious, doubtful and unbelieving thoughts. May I give way to no direct murmurings, no repinings at the prosperity of others, no harsh reflections on Providence, but may I maintain a constant acknowledgement of your justice and goodness. Save me from thinking severely or unjustly of others, from being too much dejected or disposed to peevishness, covetousness or negligence in affairs, from working too much or too little.[464]

Susanna Wesley

Prayer offering thanks

22

Lord, when my eye confronts my heart, and I realise that you have filled my heart with your love, I am breathless with amazement. Once my heart was so small in its vision, so narrow in its compassion, so weak in its zeal for truth. Then you chose to enter my heart, and now in my heart I can see you. I can love all your people, and I have the courage to proclaim the truth of your gospel to anyone and everyone. Like wax before a fire, my heart has melted under the heat of your love.[465]

Nicholas von Zinzendorf

Prayers offering commitment

23

Whatever my hands find to do, I will do it with all my might. When I have an opportunity, therefore, I will thankfully and vigorously make use of it… Saviour, I remember that when on earth you went about doing good. I must also do what good I can, especially to the souls God has committed to my care, and help me not to be discouraged by infirmities or [other] work. [466]

Susanna Wesley

24

To you, O God… my creator, redeemer and sanctifier, I give myself up entirely…

I give you my understanding : may it be my only care to know you…

I give you my will: may I have no will of my own… delighting to do your will…

I give you my affections:… what you love, may I love; what you hate, may I hate…

I give you my body : may I neither indulge it, nor use too much rigour towards it; but keep it, as far as in me lies, healthy, vigorous, and active, and fit to do you all manner of service…

I give you all my worldly goods : may I prize them and use them only for you…

I give you my… reputation : may I never value it but only in respect… as it may do you service…

I give you myself and my all. [467] *John Wesley*

Statue of John Wesley in St Paul's Churchyard, London

25

Lord, help me to begin to begin.[468] *George Whitefield*

26

Glory be to you, O triune God. I desire to be wholly yours forever. This day I give myself up to you as a living sacrifice… I leave to your management and direction all that I possess and all that I wish. I set every enjoyment and interest before you to be disposed of as you please. Although I dare not say that

I will never complain, yet I will labour not only to submit but also to acquiesce to your will. I will not only bear the heaviest afflictions on me but I will also consent to them, and praise you for them, contentedly resolving my will into yours… Destroy, I beseech you, the power of sin in my heart more and more, and transform me more into the image of Jesus… Grant to me all the needful influences of your purifying, cheering, and comforting Spirit, and lift up that light of your countenance upon me that will put the greatest joy and gladness into my heart. Dispose of my affairs, O God, in a manner that will be wholly useful to your glory and my own true happiness… I desire to live and die with my hand upon the hope of eternal life… Amen.[469]

William Grimshaw

Stained glass window of Charles Wesley in New Room Archives and Library

27

Forth in your name, O Lord, I go,
my daily labour to pursue;
you, only you, resolved to know
in all I think, or speak, or do.

The task your wisdom has assigned,
O let me cheerfully fulfill;
in all my works your presence find,
and prove your good and perfect will…

Give me to bear your easy yoke,
and every moment watch and pray,
and still to things eternal look,
and hasten to your glorious day.

For you delightfully employ
whatever your bounteous grace has given;

and run my course with even joy,
and closely walk with you to Heaven.[470]   *Charles Wesley*

28

My prayer today is that God will make me an extraordinary Christian.[471]   *George Whitefield*

29

O Lord, open my eyes that I may see the footsteps of Jesus and tread in all his righteous ways, turning neither to the right hand or the left, but keep in that path which ends in everlasting life. Amen.[472]   *Susanna Designe*

30

I am no longer my own, but yours. Put me to what you will, rank me with whom you will; put me to doing, put me to suffering; let me be employed for you or laid aside for you, exalted for you or brought low for you; let me be full, let me be empty; let me have all things, let me have nothing; I freely and heartily yield all things to your pleasure and disposal.[473]   *John Wesley*

31

Take my soul and body's powers;
take my memory, mind and will;
all my goods, and all my hours;
all I know and all I feel;
all I think, or speak or do;
take my heart, but make it new.[474]   *Charles Wesley*

Prayers for worship on Sunday

32

Statue of John Wesley outside Wesley's Chapel in City Road, London

This is is your day: O Lord enable me to rejoice and be glad in it. May I ever remember to keep this day holy, not doing my own tasks, nor finding my own pleasures... [but using the time] for the instruction of my mind, for the reforming my life and the saving my soul... Increase my love for your word, and enable me to hear it meekly and receive it with pure affection so it may bring forth the fruit of good living. Open my understanding to receive your truth... set it so powerfully in my heart and root it so deep in my soul that its fruit may be seen in my life to your glory and praise... Amen.[475]   *John Wesley*

33

O Lord God, I thank you for all the blessings and favours... so freely bestowed on me... You have been exceedingly good and kind to me beyond all that I had reason to expect, or I am able to express... I bless you that your house is open to me, the bread of life is offered to me, and the word of salvation is preached... Do not let your word be lost on me. Apply it to my heart and fix it in my memory that it may prove a blessing... Pardon my neglects and the guilt of my misdoings... and help me walk more worthily... Above all, O blessed God, give me a heart filled with your love, lifted up in praise, and devoted to your honour and glory all the days of my life.'[476]   *John Wesley*

Prayer for a sick friend

34

See, gracious Lord, with pitying eyes,
my friend who now a sufferer lies…
his sickness feel, endure his pain,
his burden bear, his cross sustain,
grieve in his griefs and sigh in his sighs…
enter his heart, possess him whole.[477]   *Charles Wesley*

A parents' prayer for their children

35

Your hand beneficent extend
to bless, and shelter, and defend;
your Spirit to my children give
and let them to your glory live. [478]   *Charles Wesley*

Prayer for others

36

God, we pray to you for all the dark corners of the earth, for all who are suffering under the evil of slavery, or from injustice or cruelty of any kind… Let it not be said that I was silent when they needed me.[479]

William Wilberforce

William Wilberforce by Karl Anton Hickel (Wilberforce House Museum)

Prayers for empowerment

37

O Lord, incline my ears to wisdom, and my heart to understanding, that I may… increase in the knowledge and love of God… Let all my powers be employed to your glory.[480]

John Wesley

38

O Lord God Almighty…

I praise and bless your holy name for all your goodness and loving kindness to all humanity.

I bless you for our creation, our preservation, and all the blessings of this life;

but above all, for your great love in the redemption of the world by our Lord Jesus Christ.

I bless you… for bringing me safe to the beginning of a new day…

Grant that this day I may fall into no sin, neither run into any kind of danger…

Keep me, I beseech you, O Lord, from all things hurtful to my soul or body,

and grant me your pardon and peace,

so that, being cleansed from all my sins,

I might serve you with a quiet mind… and continue in the same until my life's end,

through Jesus Christ, my Saviour and Redeemer. Amen. [481]

John Wesley

39

While I am a pilgrim here,
let your love my spirit cheer;

be my guide, my guard, my friend,
lead me to my journey's end.
Show me what I have to do;
every hour my strength renew.[482]

John Newton

John Newton (New Room Archives and Library)

40

Gracious Lord… Be you light to my eyes, music to my ears, sweetness to my taste, and full contentment to my heart. Be you my sunshine in the day, my food at the table, my repose in the night… Grant me sorrow for my sins, thankfulness for my benefits, fear of your judgments, love of your mercies, and mindfulness of your presence… Make me loving to my friends and charitable to my enemies. Give me modesty in my countenance, gravity in my behaviour, deliberation in my speech, holiness in my thoughts, and righteousness in all my actions. Let your mercy cleanse me from my sins, and your grace bring forth in me the fruits of everlasting life… May I seek to know thy will, and, when I know it, may I perform it faithfully to the honour and glory of your ever-blessed name. Amen.[483]

Elizabeth Rhodes

41

O you who came from above,
the pure celestial fire to impart,
kindle a flame of sacred love
on the mean altar of my heart.

There let it for your glory burn
with inextinguishable blaze,
and trembling to its source return,
in humble prayer and fervent praise.

Jesus, confirm my heart's desire
to work and speak and think for you.
Still let me guard the holy fire,
and still stir up your gift in me.

Ready for all your perfect will,
my acts of faith and love repeat,
until death your endless mercies seal,
and make my sacrifice complete.[484]   *Charles Wesley*

42

Lord… may all the happenings of my life prove useful and beneficial to me. May all things instruct me and then afford me opportunity of exercising some virtue and daily learning and growing toward your likeness, let the world go which way it will.[485]   *Susanna Wesley*

43

Holy God whose nature and name is Love…
seeing as there is in Christ Jesus an infinite fullness of all that we can want or wish,
may we all receive of his fullness, grace upon grace;
grace to pardon our sins and subdue our iniquities;
grace to justify our persons and to sanctify our souls;
grace to complete that holy change, that renewal of our hearts,
whereby we may be transformed into the blessed image wherein you did create us…

restrain us from the sins into which we are most prone to fall, and quicken us to the duties we are most averse to perform; and grant that we may think and speak and will and do the things becoming the children of our heavenly Father... Amen.[486]

John Wesley

44

God, I give you praise for days well spent, but I am yet unsatisfied... I would have my soul more closely united to you by faith and love. You know, Lord, that I would love you above all things. You know me, you know my desires, my expectations... It is your favour, your acceptance, the communications of your grace, that I earnestly wish for more than anything else in the world. [487]

Susanna Wesley

Prayers for the family

45

Deliver us from worldly cares and foolish desires, from vain hopes and causeless fears... We resign ourselves to your wisdom and goodness. You know what is best for us. [488]

John Wesley

John Wesley by Frank Salisbury 1932 (Museum of Methodism)

46

O God... Seeing there is in Jesus an infinite fullness of all that we can want or wish, may we all receive of his fullness, grace upon grace, grace to pardon our sins and subdue our iniquities... grace to sanctify our souls and to complete that holy change, that renewal of our hearts, whereby we may be transformed... Restrain us from the sins into which we are most prone to fall, and quicken us to the duties we are most averse to perform; and grant that we may think and speak, and will and do things becoming the children of the heavenly Father.[489]   *John Wesley*

Prayer for the family of the Church

47

Christ, from whom all blessings flow,
perfecting the saints below,
hear us, who your nature share,
who your mystic body are.

Join us, in one spirit join…
nourish us, O Christ, and feed;
let us daily growth receive,
more and more in Jesus live…

Move and actuate and guide,
diverse gifts to each divide;
placed according to your will,
let us all our work fulfill. [490]   *Charles Wesley*

*Charles Wesley depicted in stained glass window
at Grace United Methodist Church in Atlanta*

Prayers for lay preachers

48

Jesus, your servants bless,
who sent by you proclaim
the peace and joy and righteousness
experienced in your name...
Our souls with faith supply,
with life and liberty...
We live for this alone:
your grace to minister;
and all you have for sinners done
in life and death declare.[491]

Charles Wesley

49

O give me now to speak your word
in this appointed hour;
attend it with your Spirit, Lord,
and let it come with power.[492]

Charles Wesley

Prayer of praise

50

I would speak magnificently of you, Almighty God, the high
and mighty one, the creator who inhabits eternity. I would speak
magnificently and more worthily of you. You are immense,
infinitely perfect... Holiness is your essence... There is no
contrariness or contradiction in you, no variableness or shadow
of turning. You are power, wisdom, justice, goodness and truth.
You are perfection of being, who comprehends all and infinitely
more than we can possibly conceive. You are essential glory. [493]

Susanna Wesley

Prayers before a meal

51

Glory, love, and praise and honour
for our food
now bestowed.[494]　　　　　　*Charles Wesley*

52

We thank Thee, Lord, for this our food,
for life and health and every good;
by your own hand may we be fed;
give us each day our daily bread.[495]　　*John Cennick*

*A Wesley Teapot, one of many mass produced from an original
teapot designed for Wesley by Josiah Wedgwood*

Prayers before bedtime

53

God, accept my sincere praise and thanksgiving for all the
blessings and mercies that I have enjoyed this day… Give your

angels charge over me, and grant me such rest and sleep as may fit me for tomorrow's duties… Amen.[496] *John Wesley*

54

With your protection blessed,
calm I lay me down to rest [497] *Charles Wesley*

55

Under the shadow of your wings let me pass this night in comfort and peace. Keep me both in body and soul, and give me as much rest as my body has need of. [498] *John Wesley*

John and Charles Wesley depicted in stained glass window at Wesley's Chapel in London

---

A final benediction

56

May the grace of Christ our Saviour
and the Father's boundless love,
with the Holy Spirit's favour,
rest upon us from above
Thus may we abide in union
with each other and the Lord,
and possess in sweet communion,
joys which earth cannot afford.[499]

John Newton

57

Now, to God the Father, who first loved us, and made us accepted in the Beloved;
to God the Son, who loved us, and washed us from our sins in his own blood;
to God the Holy Spirit, who sheds the love of God abroad in our hearts,
be all love and all glory in time and to all eternity.[500]

John Wesley

Further Reading

There have been thousands of books written on Methodism, especially on John Wesley. The very brief list of recommended books below is designed not for the historical specialist but for the general reader who wishes to know more, although I have included some academic studies:

On early Methodism

I unashamedly would recommend my book 'The Cradle of Methodism' (2017 New Room Publishing) as being now the best introduction to early Methodism, even though its chief focus is on Bristol and Kingswood. Since its publication it has been much acclaimed for both its research and its readability. One reviewer described it as an a history that is unexpectedly page-turning. Academic books on early Methodism abound, of which I think the most memorable of the more recent ones are *The Evangelical Conversion Narrative* by Bruce Hindmarsh (2008 OUP) and *The Elect Methodists: Calvinistic Methodism in England and Wales 1735-1811* by David Ceri Jones, Boyd S. Schlenther and Eryn M. White (2012 Univ of Wales Press). For the general reader I would recommend reading one or more of the following: *The Making of Methodism* by Barrie Tabraham (1995 Epworth Press), *The Rise of Evangelicanism* by Mark A. Noll 2004 (IVP), and *Wesley and the People Called Methodists* by Richard Heitzenrater (2013 second edition Abingdon Press). Also still worth looking at if you can find second-hand copies are the two books by Leslie Church: *The Early Methodist People* (1948 Epworth Press) and *More about the early Methodist People* (1949 Epworth Press).

On John Wesley:

There are a number of different multi-volumed editions of the complete works of John Wesley (the best is the Bicentennial Edition), but for the general reader there is no better introduction than reading a simple selection from his *Journal* (providing you bear in mind it helped create the myth that he was single-handedly responsible for the creation of the Methodist movement). An easily accessible edition is F.H. Revell's selection originally produced in 1903 but reprinted in 2016. The most highly respected academic biography on Wesley is probably still *Reasonable Enthusiast: John Wesley and the Rise of Methodism* by Henry Rack (1989 and third edition 2014 Epworth Press). The most readable of the modern 'popular' biographies are, in my opinion, *A Brand Plucked from the Burning* by Roy Hattersley (2002 Little Brown) and *John Wesley: A Personal Portrait* by Ralph Waller (2003 OUP), although some people may like the straightforward style of *John Wesley* by Stephen Tomkins (2003 Lion Publishing). *On The Trail of John Wesley* by K. Cheetham (2003 Luath) provides an interesting look at Wesley's life based on the places he visited. For sheer readability I would also recommend the much older *Burning Heart: John Wesley Evangelist* by Arthur Skevington Wood (1968 Paternoster Press), although some of his judgements would no longer be supported by modern research. His *'The Inextinguishable Blaze'* (1967 Paternoster Press), which covers the evangelical revival in the eighteenth century, is an equally good read. If you want to focus on the social justice issues I would recommend the more academic *The Poor and the People Called Methodists* edited by Richard Heitzenrater (2002 Kingswood Books).

On Charles Wesley:

After decades of neglect research on Charles is blossoming and new editions of his sermons, letters, poetry and journal have appeared in the last ten years. Particularly notable is *The Manuscript Journal of the Rev. Charles Wesley* edited by S.T. Kimbrough and Kenneth

Newport (2 volumes 2007 Kingswood Books). By far the most readable of the modern biographies are my book *Charles Wesley* (2007 Epworth Press) and *Assist Me To Proclaim* by John R. Tyson (2007 Eerdmans), but some might also find helpful the older *The Man with the Dancing Heart* by T. Crichton Mitchell (1994 Beacon Hill Press) or, in the series *Exploring Methodism*, *Brother Charles* by Barrie Tabraham (2003 Epworth Press). If you want just a simple introduction I would recommend my booklet *Charles Wesley* (2014 New Room Publications). If you want a taste of the modern research being undertaken on Charles there is an interesting but academic selection in *Charles Wesley: Life, Literature and Legacy* edited by Kenneth Newport and Ted Campbell (2011 Epworth Press) and aspects of Charles' life are covered well in *Charles Wesley and the Struggle for Methodist Identity* by Gareth Lloyd (2007 OUP). I think the definitive academic study on his hymns remains *The Evangelical Doctrines of Charles Wesley's Hymns* by Ernest Rattenbury (1954 Epworth Press) but, if you are very interested in hymns generally, I would recommend reading *The English Hymn: A Critical and Historical Study* by J.R. Watson (1991 OUP) and *Music and the Wesleys* by Nicholas Temperley and Stephen Banfield (2010 Univ. of Illinois Press) or the far more accessible *O Sing Unto the Lord: A History of English Church Music* (2015 Profile Books).

On George Whitefield:

Like the Wesleys, there have been new editions of Whitefield's complete works produced in recent years (notably by the Quinta Press). Although largely neglected by British historians (except for a few notable exceptions), Whitefield has been extensively written about by American scholars and there are many biographies of him. In my opinion the best short introduction is *George Whitefield: Evangelist of the Eighteenth Century Revival* by Arnold Dallimore (2000 Evangelical Press) which is a summary of his fascinating two-volume biography published by the Banner of Truth Trust in 1980. If you are very enthusiastic, there is the monumental (over a 1,000 pages!) *George Whitefield: A Definitive Biography* by E.A. Johnston (2007 Tentmaker Publications). Modern research on him is best covered in a series of articles published in *George Whitefield: Life, Context, and Legacy* edited by Geordan Hammond and David Ceri Jones (2016 OUP) and in two new biographies: *George Whitefield: America's Spiritual Founding Father* by Thomas Kidd (2016 Yale Univ. Press) and *George Whitefield: Evangelist for God and Empire* by Peter Choi (2018 Eerdmans).

On other eighteenth-century evangelical clergy:
There are two readable biographies of William Grimshaw: *Wiliam Grimshaw* by Frank Baker (1963 Epworth Press) and *William Grimshaw of Haworth* by Faith Cook (1997 Banner of Truth Trust). The best academic book on Fletcher is *Reluctant Saint* by Patrick Streiff (2001 Epworth Press), although its emphasis is on his theology and it lacks some of the insights provided in *Unexampled Labours: Letters of the Revd John Fletcher to Leaders of the Evangelical Revival* by Peter Forsaith (2008 Epworth Press). There is a website called 'The Fletcher Page' dedicated to Fletcher and his wife Mary Bosanquet. Benjamin Ingham as yet lacks a major biography, although there have been a number of articles written on him and his Oxford diary has been edited and published. The best available book on him is still the readable but rather superficial *Benjamin Ingham* by H.M. Pickles (1995 H.M. Pickles, Coventry). I think the best book on Thomas Coke remains *Thomas Coke: Apostle of Methodism* by John Vickers (1969 Epworth Press and reprinted 2013 Wipf & Stock). A variety of books have been published on other evangelical clergy of the eighteenth century who had varying degrees of contact with Methodism. The most covered is John Newton because of his authorship of 'Amazing Grace' and involvement in the slavery issue.

The best academic study is probably *John Newton and the English Evangelical Tradition* by Bruce Hindmarsh (2000 Eerdmans), but I would recommend for the general reader *John Newton* by Jonathan Aitken (2013 Crossway Books).

On the Lay Preachers:

In the nineteenth century there were various editions produced of edited or transcribed versions of   the autobiographical accounts produced by some of the lay preachers and, if you can find a copy of the versions produced by Thomas Jackson in c1865 or George Stevenson in c1886 or John Telford in c1913 or look at them online, they still make for interesting reading. The excellent *John Wesley's Preachers* by John Lenton (2008 Paternoster Press) provides a fascinating modern statistical analysis of the preachers but does not provide accounts of their lives. The Welsh interest has ensured that Howell Harris has been much written about. I think the best book on him is *Howell Harris: From Conversion to Separation* by Geraint Tudor (2002 Univ of Wales Press) but it only covers the period 1735-1750. Harris' own short account of his life is worth reading and it is available in a modern reprint (*Howell Harris' Story* 2015 White Tree Publishing). Sadly there are no well-researched modern biographies of other lay preachers except for my well-received biography *John Cennick: The Forgotten Evangelist* (2016 New Room Publications) and *John Bennet and the Origins of Methodism and the Evangelical Revival* by S.R. Valentine (1997 Scarecrow Press). The lay preachers connected to American Methodism have received more study, especially Francis Asbury. The best modern book on him is *American Saint: Francis Asbury and the Methodists* by John Wigger (2009 OUP) . Those interested in Captain Webb should read the booklet Captain Thomas Webb by Ralph Bates (originally published in 1975 and reprinted by New Room Publications). For a wider but academic look read *The Methodists and Revolutionary America*

1760-1800 by Dee Andrews (2000 Princetown Univ. Press).

On the early Methodist women:

A number of interesting books on the role of women have appeared in the last decade and a number of edited selections from the writings of early Methodist women are now in print. The best are in *Her Own Story* by Paul W. Chilcote (2001 Kingswood Books) and *Early Methodist Spirituality* by Paul W. Chilcote (2007 Kingswood Books). His *John Wesley and the women preachers of early Methodism* (1991 Scarecrow Press) is also very useful. From my perspective the most interesting academic study is *Heart Religion in the British Enlightenment* by Phylis Mack (2008 Cambridge). The two women who have most been written about are Susanna Wesley and Selina Hastings, Countess of Huntingdon. An excellent edition of Susanna's complete writings was produced by Charles Wallace in 1997 (OUP) and, since that appeared, numerous selections of her prayers and other writings have appeared. A very good introduction to her life can be found in my booklet *Susanna Wesley* (2014 New Room Publishing) but the best full biography remains *Susanna Wesley and the Puritan Tradition in Methodism* by John A. Newton (1968 Epworth Press). Readers might also find interesting my booklet on the Wesley sisters: *The Seven Sisters* (2011 New Room Publishing). There are many biographies available on the Countess of Huntingdon, including a modern re-assessment of her life in *Spiritual Pilgrim* by Edwin Welch (2013 Univ of Wales Press) but I think the most readable book for the general reader remains *Selina: Countess of Huntingdon* by Faith Cook (2001 Banner of Truth). For those wanting a biographical approach to other figures, such as Sarah Crosby, Hannah Ball, Mary Fletcher, etc, the best short book remains the out-of-print *Early Methodist Women* by Thomas Morrow (1967 Epworth Press) if you can find a copy. Only two of the female lay preachers, Mary Bosanquet Fletcher and Grace

Murray have full-scale biographies in print : an 1817 biography of the former by Henry Moore has been reprinted for internet sales and I have written a new modern biography on the latter: *Grace Murray: the woman whom Wesley loved and lost* (2016 New Room Publishing). I have been very pleased by the acclaim given to my book on Grace.

Online resources and visiting heritage sites

It is worth going on the Wesley Historical Society site (www. wesleyhistoricalsociety.org.uk) for access to the online Dictionary of Methodism and on the Methodist Heritage website (www. methodistheritage.org.uk) for details of the many other online resources now available. See its 'researching Methodist history' section. The Methodist Heritage site also provides details of the many heritage sites in the U.K. (and you can order a free Methodist Heritage Handbook and sign up for the Methodist Heritage newsletter). Anyone who is really interested in John and Charles Wesley should try if at all possible to visit the sites associated with them, particularly what might be termed 'the big three': the Epworth Rectory, Wesley's Chapel and John Wesley's House in London with its associated Museum of Methodism, and, above all, the New Room and Charles Wesley's House in Bristol with its associated Museum. All these three sites have their own websites where you can obtain more information on visiting times, etc (www.epwortholdrectory. org.uk. ; www.wesleyschapel.org.uk ; and www.newroombristol.org. uk).

I would make a particular plea for you to visit the Museum at the New Room which opened in 2017. It contains many interesting items and is dedicated to telling the story of the Wesleys in a very dynamic and interactive way (as some of the photographs in this book illustrate). It has been much praised, not least because it shows the continued relevance of the Wesleys for today's world in thought-provoking ways. The Secretary of the Wesley Historical Society has described it as 'quite simply the best introduction Methodism now has to offer to its eighteenth-century origins and impact and it deserves to be made widely known within and beyond Methodism'.

Proceeds from the sale of this book will go towards maintaining the work of the New Room in Bristol.

Sources

1   Letter to Samuel Annesley 20 Jan 1720.
2   From sermon published in *A continuation of morning exercise questions ... resolved by sundry ministers* 1682.
3   Letter to her husband 6 Feb 1712.
4   Words spoken when Samuel was forcing her sister Hetty to marry an unsuitable husband.
5   Quoted from her writings in S.Pellowe: *A Wesley Family Book of Days* 1994.
6   Quoted in Eliza Clarke *Susanna Wesley* 1876.
7   Letter to JW 8 June 1725.
8   Letter to her daughter Sukey 13 Jan 1710.
9   Letter to her eldest son Samuel Oct 1709.
10 From 'Peace and unity more important than the triumph of your opinion' in *Susanna Wesley: The Complete Writings* 1997.
11 Preface to his *Sermons on Several Occasions* 1746.
12 CW *Journal* 16 Sept 1739.
13 Letter to Samuel Wesley Jr 14 Feb 1709.
14 Her *Journal* 17 May 1711.
15 'Public Schools' in *Edinburgh Review* 1810.
16 *Memoirs of the Wesley Family from original documents* 1823.
17 From manuscript 'Miscellaneous Hymns' John Ryland's Library, Manchester.
18 *Memoirs of the Wesley family from original documents* 1823.
19 Reflecting on his lifestyle in his diary 26 March 1725.
20 *Memoirs of my life and writings* 1796.
21 Letter to JW March 1726.
22 See T. Jackson T*he Life of the Rev Charles Wesley* Vol I 1841 pg 14.
23 Recalled 50 years later in Sermon 105: *On Conscience* 1788.
24 Letter to JW and CW 5 July 1727.
25 Letter to his father 14 Jan 1734.
26 Letter to JW and CW 28 April 1731.
27 *Methodist Magazine* 1798.
28 *A Short Account of God's Dealings with the Rev. George Whitefield from his Infancy to the time of his entering Holy Orders* 1773.
29 Letter to his father.
30 Attributed to JW (probably based on phrase in *A Plain Account of Christian Perfection* 1777).
31 Lines from 'Weary of wandering from my God' in *Hymns and Sacred Poems* 1749.
32 Preface to *Sermons on Several Occasions* 1746.
33 From 'Christ himself the precept gives' in collection of hymns based on John's gospel 1763.
34 Summarised version from original guidelines.
35 Letter to Mary Bishop 11 Feb 1775.
36 Lines from 'O for a 1,000 tongues to sing' in *Hymns And Sacred Poems* 1740.
37 *A Plain Account of the People Called Methodists* 1748.
38 Lines from 'Help us to help each other, Lord' in *Hymns and Sacred Poems* 1742.
39 Sermon 101: *The Duty of Constant Communion* 1732.
40 Lines from 'O the Depth of Love Divine' in *Hymns on the Lord's Supper* 1745.
41 Sermon 27: *Upon our Lord's Sermon on the Mount: Discourse Seven* 1747.
42 Sermon 100: *On pleasing all men* 1787 .
43 From 'A charge to keep I have' in *Short Hymns on Select Passages of Scripture* Vol I 1762.
44 Letter to eldest brother Samuel 30 April 1735.
45 Letter to CW from his eldest brother 11 Oct 1735.
46 Letter to his mother quoted in L. Tyerman: *The Life & Times of the Rev John Wesley* Vol. I pg 121-2.
47 Commonly attributed to him.
48 Commonly attributed to him, though some versions contain phrases that clearly stem from a later period.
49 JW *Journal* 25 Jan 1736.
50 CW *Journal* 30 March 1736.
51 CW's *Journal* 2 Aug 1736.
52 *Hymns and Spiritual Songs* 1707.
53 Manuscript transcribed in *Works of JW* Vol 18 1988 (Abingdon Press).
54 Words recorded by Wesley in *Journal* 22 June 1736.
55 *A Further Account of God's dealings with the Rev. George Whitefield* 1747.
56 JW *Journal* 24 Jan 1738.
57 JW *Journal* 4 March 1738.
58 JW *Journal* 23 March 1738.
59 From 'And Can It Be' in *Psalms and Hymns* 1738.
60 Sermon preached at the Church of St Mary the Virgin in Oxford 11 June 1738.
61 JW *Journal* 24 May 1738.
62 Letter to the Moravians 27-8 September 1738.
63 Sermon on 1 John 3:14 in K.Newport *The Sermons of Charles Wesley* 2001.
64 CW *Journal* 18/19 July 1738.
65 CW*Journal* 21 Oct 1738.
66 JW *Journal* 1 Jan 1739.
67 Quoted in A.C.H. Seymour *The Life and Times of the Countess of Huntingdon* 1840.
68 GW *Journal* 17 Feb 1739.
69 *Works of John Fletcher* Vol II 1806 pg 38.
70 Letter to James Pierpoint 24 Oct 1740.
71 Letter 23 May 1740 in *Early Methodist Volume* John Ryland's Library, Manchester.
72 GW *Journal* 7 March 1739.
73 Letter to JW 3 March 1739.
74 JW *Journal* 31 March 1739.
75 JW *Journal* 2 April 1739.
76 Memoir of a Bristol clerk in *Methodist Magazine* Vol XXX 1807.
77 Letter to CW 24 May 1742.
78 Transcribed from manuscript in P.W. Chilcote *Her Own Story* 2001.
79 JW *Journal* 9 May 1739.

80   *Memoirs of James Hutton* 1856.
81   Quoted in L. Tyerman *The Life of the Rev. George Whitefield* Vol 1 1876.
82   Letter to JW 16 April 1739.
83   JW *Journal* 11 June 1739.
84   CW *Journal* 24 June 1739.
85   *A Discourse on Faith and Hope in the Gospel* 1763.
86   GW *Journal* 6/7 and 10 July 1739.
87   Letter to Rev RD 10 Nov 1739.
88   Benjamin Franklin's *Autobiography* 1793
89   Benjamin Franklin's *Autobiography* 1793
90   *Explanatory Notes on the New Testament* 1754.
91   *An Earnest Appeal to Men of Reason and Religion* 1743.
92   JW *Journal* 16 June 1755.
93   Sermon 14: *The Repentance of Believers* 1758.
94   Sermon 82: *On Temptation* 1786.
95   Hymn on Zechariah 4: 7 in *Hymns and Sacred Poems* 1742.
96   Letter to CW 24 May 1742.
97   Letter to CW April/May1742.
98   Letter to CW April/May 1742.
99   Letter to Mary Bishop 26 Jan 1774.
100 Letter from early convert in Bristol to CW 13 April 1742.
101 From 'Come, Ye Weary Sinners, Come' in *Hymns for those that seek, and those that have Redemption in the Blood of Christ* 1747.
102 Sermon 120: *On the Wedding Garment* 1790.
103 Sermon: *The Gift and Office of the Holy Ghost* 1740.
104 Sermon 1: *Salvation by Faith* 1736.
105 From 'Where shall my wondering soul begin' in *Hymns and Sacred Poems* 1739.
106 Sermon: *The Cries of the Son of God* 1739.
107 Letter to CW 18 March 1742.
108 From 'And Can It Be' in *Psalms and Hymns* 1738.
109 From 'Happy the souls to Jesus joined' in *Hymns on the Lord's Supper* 1745.
110 *Principles of A Methodist Farther Explained* 1746.
111 Letter to CW April/May 1742.
112 K. Newport: *Sermons of CW* 2001
113 From 'Forth in Thy Name' in *Hymns and Sacred Poems* 1749.
114 Sermon 2: *The Almost Christian* 1741.
115 From 'Love divine, all loves excelling' in *Hymns for those that seek, and those that have Redemption* 1747.
116 From 'Author of faith, eternal Word' in *Hymns and Sacred Poems* 1740.
117 *Memoir of Hannah Ball* 5 Dec 1779.
118 *A Farther Appeal to Men of Reason and Religion* 1745.
119 Letter to CW April/May1742.
120 From 'All things are possible' in *Hymns and Sacred Poems* 1749.
121 From 'My God I am thine' in *Hymns and Sacred Poems* 1749.
122 1740 manuscript in *Early Methodist Volume*, John Ryland's Library, Manchester.
123 1741 manuscript in *Early Methodist Volume*, John Ryland's Library, Manchester.
124 Letter to John Smith 25 March 1747.
125 Letter to Robert Brackenbury 20 Oct 1787.
126 Sermon 50: *The Use of Money* 1780.
127 Cited in M.Water *The New Encyclopaedia of Christian Quotation*s 2000
128 From 'Love divine, all loves excelling' in *Hymns for those that seek and those that have Redemption* 1747.
129 Sermon 125: *On living without God* 1790.
130 Sermon 82: *On Temptation* 1786.
131 Sermon 24: *Upon the Lord's Sermon on the Mount: Discourse Four* 1740.
132 Attributed to John Wesley. It is now thought to be a summary of his teaching produced after his death.
133 Sermon 69: *The Imperfection of Human Knowledge* 1784.
134 From 'Lord that I may learn of you' in *Short Hymns on Select Passages of Scripture* 1762.
135 From 'Let Earth and Heaven combine' in *Hymns for the Nativity of Our Lord* 1745.
136 From 'O for a heart to love my God' in *Hymns and Sacred Poems*1742.
137 From 'A charge to keep I have' in *Short Hymns on Select Passages of Scripture* 1762
138 Letter to society members at Bristol 29 Oct 1741
139 From 'All praise to our redeeming Lord' in *Hymns for those that seek and those that have found Redemption* 1747
140 *A Plain Account of Christian Perfection* 1766
141 Letter to Ann Loxdale 30 June 1779.
142 *An account of the death of Sarah Lawrence* in 1800 published 1820.
143 *An account of death of Sarah Crosby* in *Methodist Magazine* 1806.
144 From 'Come let us join our friends above' in *Funeral Hymns* 1759.
145 From manuscript written by JW in John Ryland's Library, Manchester.
146 JW *Journal* 30 April 1739.
147 Letter to the 'Ministers called Methodists' 31 May 1740.
148 Letter to JW 25 June 1739.
149 Quoted in E. Evans: *The Evangelical Spirituality of Howell Harris* 2006.
150 JW *Journal* 7 June 1739.
151 CW *Journal* 31 Aug 1739.
152 His account transcribed in *Proceedings of Wesley Historical Society* Vol 42 1980.
153 Hymn for the Kingswood Colliers in *Hymns and Sacred Poems* 1740.
154 *Short Narrative of the chief particulars of the life of the Revd Mr John Cennick* 1755.
155 From Hymn 1 in *Sacred Hymns for the Children of God in the days of their pilgrimage* 1742.
156 CW *Journal* 28 Sept 1739.
157 Letter to Dr Doddridge 23 Feb 1747.
158 *A Plain Account of the People called Methodists* 1748.
159 Sermon 95: *On the Education of Children* 1783.
160 This was phrase he often used.
161 Sermon 128: *Free Grace* 1739.
162 JW *Journal* 23 Oct 1739.

163 Letter to JW 16 July 1740.
164 CW *Journal* 6 Aug 1740.
165 Letter to CW April/May 1742.
166 CW *Journal* 22 Sept 1740.
167 *A Plain Account of the People Called Methodists* 1748
168 The complete poem is in T. Jackson *Life of Rev Charles Wesley* Vol II 1841.
169 John Nelson's *Journal* 17 June 1739.
170 *Humphrey Clinker* 1771.
171 Quoted in J. Hutton *History of the Moravian Church* 1909.
172 CW *Journal* 25 April 1740.
173 CW *Journal* 22 June 1740.
174 Letter to GW 1 Sept 1740.
175 Proposed letter that Charles drafted 6 Dec 1740 .
176 *An Account of the most remarkable occurrences in the awakenings at Bristol and Kingswood till the Brethren's labours began there in 1746* published 1750.
177 Quoted in J.E.Hutton, *John Cennick: A Sketch* 1909
178 *An Account of the most remarkable occurrences in the awakenings at Bristol and Kingswood till the Brethren's labours began there in 1746* published1750.
179 *A Plain Account of Christian Perfection* 1766 and letter to Miss A. 14 Oct 1767.
180 *A Plain Account of Christian Perfection* 1766.
181 *A Plain Account of Christian Perfection* 1766.
182 From hymn based on Matthew 18:6.
183 JW *Journal* 26 Dec 1740.
184 Letter quoted in JW *Journal* 22 Feb 1741.
185 Letter to JW 28 Feb 1741.
186 *An Account of the most remarkable occurrences in the awakenings at Bristol and Kingswood till the Brethren's labours began there in 1746* published 1750.
187 Quoted in Rev. L. Tyerman *Life and Times of John Wesley* Vol 1 1856.
188 Letter to JW 10 March 1741.
189 From his account of his life edit T. Jackson *The Lives of the Early Methodist Preachers* Vol II 1866.
190 Letter to JW 10 Oct 1741.
191 From 'Free Grace' in *Hymns of God's Everlasting Love* 1741.
192 *An Epistle to the Rev George Whitefield* 1775.
193 Quoted in L. Tyerman: *Life of George Whitefield* Vol I.
194 *A Plain Account of the People Called Methodists* 1746.
195 *The Character of a Methodist* 1742.
196 *Some remarks on a letter from the Rev. Mr Whitefield to the Rev. Mr Wesley* 1742.
197 JW *Journal* 28-30 May 1742.
198 His account of his life edit. T. Jackson *The Lives of the Early Methodist Preachers* Vol 1 1865.
199 Letter published in Whitefield's *Weekly History* 7 Aug 1742
200 Letter to John Cennick 29 May 1742.
201 *Journal of John Nelson: Being an account of God's dealing with him from his youth* 1789.
202 *Memoirs of the Life of the late William Grimshaw* 1799.
203 Letter to the societies in Newcastle 12 Jan 1762.
204 Letter to the societies at Newcastle cited in R.A.

Hardy, *William Grimshaw* 1877.
205 Cited in R.A. Hardy, *William Grimshaw* 1877.
206 JW *Journal* 23 Dec 1742.
207 Letter to Howell Harris in G.M. Roberts *Selected Trevecka Letters 1742-7* published 1956.
208 Bennet *Journal* 3 June 1742.
209 Bennet *Journal*.
210 From Eucharistic Hymn LXXII in *Hymns on the Lord's Supper* 1745.
211 CW *Journal* 21 May 1743 on mob violence in Walsall.
212 *An Earnest Appeal to Men of Religion and Reason* 1744.
213 CW *Journal* 4 June 1743.
214 CW *Journal* 19 July 1743 on mob violence in Morva.
215 JW *Journal* 20 Oct 1743.
216 From Hymn 1 in *Hymns for Times of Trouble and Persecution* 1744.
217 Quoted in A. Dallimore *George Whitefield* Vol 1 1980.
218 Letter to CW 24 Jan 1741.
219 Letter to James Beaumont 18 Feb 1744.
220 Statement agreed at first meeting of English branch of Calvinistic Methodist Association April 1744.
221 *Arminian Magazine* 1785.
222 *Works of GW* Vol IV 1771
223 JW *Journal* 14 Feb 1745.
224 Minutes of the Second Methodist Conference 1745.
225 Letter to Mayor of Newcastle 26 Oct 1745.
226 Letter to JC 1 July 1747.
227 Quoted in *Memoirs of James Hutton* 1856.
228 CW *Journal* 2 May 1746.
229 Transcribed in L.Tyerman *Life of Rev. John Wesley* Vol I 1878.
230 *Methodist Memorial* 1801.
231 CW *Journal* 6 July 1746.
232 From 'Praise for the success of the gospel' written Dec 1746 and published in *Hymns and Sacred Poems* 1749.
233 From Hymn LXXII in *Hymns for Children* 1763.
234 *Thoughts on educating children* 1783.
235 From Hymn XL in *Hymns for Children* 1768.
236 Letter to J. Benson Nov 1768.
237 *Lessons for Children* 1746.
238 JW *Journal* 23 Feb 1749.
239 JW *Journal* 9 Feb 1748.
240 *Short Hymns on Select Passages of Sacred Scriptures* 1762.
241 Letter to Rev.Dr.Conyers Middleton 4 Jan 1749.
242 Letter 'Thoughts on the present scarcity of provisions' in *Lloyd's Evening Post* Dec 1772.
243 JW *Journal* 7 May 1741.
244 JW *Journal* 25 Nov 1740.
245 Sermon 126 *On the danger of increasing riches* 1790.
246 Sermon 50: *The Use of Money* 1744.
247 Sermon 126: *On the danger of increasing riches* 1790.
248 Taken from the annual report of the Strangers Friend Society 1835.
249 *A Plain Account of Christian Perfection* 1766.
250 Letter XXX in *The Confessions of J.Lackington, late*

Bookseller at the Temple of the Muses 1804.

251 A Plain Account of the People Called Methodists 1748.

252 JW Journal 27 Nov 1739.

253 A Plain Account of the People Called Methodists 1748.

254 Letter to Mr Blackwell 26 Jan 1747.

255 Letter to Mr S at Armagh 24 April 1769.

256 Preface to Primitive Physic 1748.

257 An Answer to a letter published in the Bath Journal 27 May 1749.

258 Letter to Felix Farley's Bristol Journal 1773.

259 JW Journal 29 Sept 1781 on visiting asylum run in Bristol by Richard Henderson.

260 JW Journal 6 Oct 1774.

261 Letter to Mayor and Corporation sent via Charles 20 Dec 1764.

262 Sermon 47: On heaviness through manifold temptations 1754.

263 Letter to Miss Furly 25 Sept 1757.

264 Sermon 98: On Visiting the Sick 1786.

265 Sermon 98: On Visiting the Sick 1786.

266 From Hymns for the use of families and on various occasions 1767.

267 Sermon 98: On visiting the Sick 1786.

268 Sermon 60: The General Deliverence 1781.

269 CW Journal 2 Aug 1736.

270 Works of GW Vol IV

271 Sermon 20: The Lord our Righteousness 1758.

272 Memoirs of Anthony Benezet 1817.

273 Thoughts Upon Slavery 1774.

274 An Account of the Life and Dealings of God with Silas Todd 1786.

275 The Interesting Narrative of the Life of Olaudah Equiano 1789.

276 Letter to CW 27 Aug 1774.

277 Memoirs of Boston King 1798.

278 Minutes of Conference 1780.

279 From Olney Hymns 1779.

280 The Negro's Complaint 1788.

281 The History of the Abolition of the Afrrican Slave Trade 1839.

282 JW Journal 6 March 1788.

283 Taken from Pity for Poor Africans published in Northampton Mercury 9 Aug 1788.

284 Letter to William Wilberforce 24 Feb 1791.

285 An account of the extraordinary conversion and religious experience of Dorothy Ripley 1817

286 Letter to Joseph Benson 5 Oct 1770

287 Quoted in A.C. H. Seymour The Life and Times of Selina, Countess of Huntingdon 1839.

288 His account of his life edit T. Jackson The Lives of the Early Methodist Preachers Vol 1 1865.

289 Elegy to Cennick written in 1761.

290 From Hymns and Sacred Poems 1749.

291 Works of GW Vol II 1771.

292 Transcription from manuscript in John Wesley's Lost Love 1910.

293 CW Journal 3 April 1748.

294 Transcription from manuscript in John Wesley's Lost Love 1910.

295 Letter to Eleanor Laroche 1769

296 Letter to Grace cited in John Wesley's Lost Love 1910.

297 Letter to Martha Hall 17 Nov 1742.

298 CW Journal 28 Oct 1749 and letter to Charles Perronet within the journal.

299 Letter to CW 20 Oct 1753.

300 Letter cited in Gillies: Works of GW Vol II 1771.

301 Quoted in Methodist Magazine 1855

302 2 Oct 1778.

303 Cited in J. Telford Wesley's Veterans Vol VI 1914.

304 Translated in Proceedings of Wesley Historical Society 1929

305 Arminian Magazine 1779.

306 Arminian Magazine 1781.

307 From 'O for a thousand tongues' in Hymns and Sacred Poems 1740.

308 From 'How can a sinner know his sins on earth forgiven' in Hymns and Sacred Poems 1749.

309 From 'Jesus! the name high over all' in Hymns and Sacred Poems 1749.

310 Preface to Select Hymns with Tunes Attached 1761.

311 From 'Meet and right it is to sing' in Hymns and Sacred Poems 1749.

312 Preface to A Collection of Hymns for the People Called Methodists 1780.

313 Preface to A Collection of Hymns for the People Called Methodists 1780.

314 Letter to Rev. Samuel Walker 21 Aug 1756.

315 CW Journal 25 Oct 1756.

316 Gillies: Works of GW Vol III 1771.

317 Part of prayer that Whitefield regularly used in praise of the Countess .

318 JW Journal 21 Sept 1761.

319 The Life of Duncan Wright written by himself 1781.

320 Letter to JW 10 Aug 1750.

321 From one of his hymns published in The Kendal Hymnbook produced by the Inghamites 1757.

322 A story he often told whilst preaching.

323 Letter to Gilbert Boyce 22 May 1750.

324 From 'Christ from whom all blessings flow' in Hymns and Sacred Poems 1740.

325 Letter to GW Dec 1763.

326 Letter to CW 11 Aug 1762.

327 Letter from lay preacher to Joseph Cownley.

328 Letter to Lady Maxwell 8 Feb 1772.

329 Letter to CW 18 Feb 1758

330 Letter to CW 11 Dec 1762.

331 Letter to the perfectionists in London 2 Nov 1762.

332 Letter signed 'Philodemus' 2 March 1763.

333 Cited in J. Telford: Wesley's Veterans 1912.

334 Letter to Joseph Cownley 1 Feb 1763 edit T. Jackson The Lives of the Early Methodist Preachers Vol II 1866.

335 Letter to CW 27 June 1766.

336 Letter to CW 15 Nov 1759.

337 1769 account translated in Proceedings of Wesley Historical Society 1929.

338 Letter to GW in The Franklin Papers Vol 16 1972.

339 Letter to Sally Wesley 21 Aug 1766.

340 Extracts from his writings in L. Tyerman Life of Rev. George Whitefield Vol II 1876.

341 JW *Journal* 28 Oct 1765.

342 Unnamed eyewitness quoted in J. Belcher, *A Biography of GW* 1857.

343 Sermon on the death of the Rev. George Whitefield 18 Nov 1770.

344 An elegy to the death of the Rev. George Whitefield 1771.

345 Letter to Alexander Mather 6 Aug 1777.

346 *Minutes of Several Conversations between the Rev John Wesley and Others 1744-91.*

347 *Minutes of Several Conversations between the Rev John Wesley and Others 1744-91.*

348 Letter to Samuel Walker 3 Sept 1756.

349 His account of his life edit. T.Jackson *The Lives of the Early Methodist Preachers* Vol 1 1865.

350 His account of his life edit. T.Jackson *The Lives of the Early Methodist Preachers* Vol 1 1865.

351 *Extract from the journal of John Nelson : being an account of God's dealing with him from his youth to the forty-second year of his age. To which is added an account of his death* 1833

352 Letter to JW 12 Nov 1779.

353 His account of his life edit T. Jackson *The Lives of the Early Methodist Preachers* Vol 1 1865.

354 Letter to preacher Robert Dall 1776 in John Ryland's Library, Manchester.

355 From 'Hymn for Husband and Wife' in S.T. Kimborough & O.A. Beckerlegge *Unpublished Poetry of CW* 1992

356 His account of his life edit T. Jackson *The Lives of the Early Methodist Preachers* Vol II 1866.

357 A poem written when the boy poet was eleven and entitled *Apostate Will.*

358 On the preacher Thomas Maxfield in J. Benson *An Apology for the People called Methodists* 1801.

359 On the preacher Joseph Humphreys in letter to Charles transcribed in *Reformation and Revival in Eighteenth-century Bristol* 1994.

360 Minutes of 1766 Conference recording questions asked of lay preacher William Ellis

361 *The Life of Thomas Taylor written by himself* edit. T. Jackson: *The Lives of the Early Methodist Preachers* Vol IV 1866.

362 Manuscript dated 26 April 1760.

363 *Life of Wesley* 1820.

364 CW *Journal* 5 Aug 1751. This was said of the preacher Michael Fenwick.

365 Letter to Samuel Walker 3 Sept 1756.

366 *The Life of Mr Duncan Wright written by himself* 1781.

367 His account of his life edit T. Jackson *The Lives of the Early Methodist Preachers* Vol V 1866

368 From diary of a book steward at the New Room now in possession of Duke University in USA.

369 *Minutes of the Methodist Conferences 1744-1798*

370 *Life of Mr Alexander Mather written by himself* in *Arminian Magazine* 1780.

371 *The Life of Mr William Ashman written by himself* 1779.

372 *A Brief Account of the Life of Howell Harris Esq.* 1791.

373 Account of his life edit T. Jackson *The Lives of the Early Methodist Preachers* Vol 1 1865.

374 Letter to JW from Rodda edit T. Jackson *The Lives of the Early Methodist Preachers* Vol II 1866.

375 Extract from his journal for 1757 in T. Jackson *The Lives of the Early Methodist Preachers* Vol III 1866.

376 *Life of Mr Robert Roberts written by himself* in letter to JW 7 July 1779.

377 JB *Journal* 9 April 1749.

378 An account of the late persecution which happened to the Brethren in Wiltshire, Whitefield's *Weekly History No* 24 19 Sept 1741.

379 His account of his life edit T. Jackson *The Lives of the Early Methodist Preachers* Vol IV 1866.

380 His account of his life edit T. Jackson *The Lives of the Early Methodist Preachers* Vol 1 1865.

381 His account of his life edit T. Jackson *The Lives of the Early Methodist Preachers* Vol I 1865.

382 *Extract from the journal of John Nelson : being an account of God's dealing with him from his youth to the forty-second year of his age. To which is added an account of his death* 1833.

383 *A Short Account of God's Dealings with Mr John Haime* 1786.

384 Letters to CW from 1741 quoted in *Methodist History* April 2003.

385 *Memoirs of Mrs Grace Bennet* edited by her son 1803.

386 Letter to Sarah Crosby in 1771 edit J. Telford *Letters of JW* Vol IV 1930.

387 Letter to JW 1771.

388 SC *Journal* 1 May 1768.

389 Letter to Sarah Mallet 15 Dec 1789.

390 Cited by John Wesley and transcribed in *John Wesley's Lost Love* 1910

391 *Memoirs of the life of Mrs Mary Taft, formerly Miss Barritt* 1828.

392 From her journal quoted in Taft : *Biographical Sketches of Holy Women* 1825.

393 *Life of Mr Richard Rodda written by himself* in *Arminian Magazine* 1784.

394 *Sermons collected in discourses on important subjects* Vol II 1801

395 JB *Journal* edited S.R.Valentine *Mirror of the Soul* 2002

396 Cited in letter to the Society of the Tabernacle 20 Oct 1743.

397 From Hymn XXIX in *Sacred Hymns for the Children of God in the days of their pilgrimage* 1741

398 Letter to JW 28 Feb 1741.

399 Letter about her husband John to JW 1762 cited in J. Lenton *John Wesley's Preachers* 2009

400 *Armenian Magazine* 1780.

401 Letter to Elizabeth Hurrell 2 July 1774.

402 Letter to JW 29 Aug 1779.

403 His account of his life edit T. Jackson *The Lives of the Early Methodist Preachers* Vol II 1866.

404 *A Brief Account of the Life of Howell Harris Esq.* 1791.

405 *Sermons collected in Discourses on Important Subjects Vol I* 1823

406 Cited in 'the Strawbridge Shrine'. Sarah was the

daughter of a neighbour converted by Strawbridge.

407 Letter to JW 11 April 1768.

408 JW *Journal* 2 Feb 1773.

409 Letter to JW 11 April 1768.

410 Pilmore's *Journal* 20 Aug 1769.

411 Pilmore's *Journal* 23 Nov 1769.

412 Minutes of 1771 Conference.

413 Asbury *Journal* 12 Sept 1771.

414 Asbury *Journal* 14 Nov 1771.

415 Quoted in M. A.Noll, *America's God* 2002.

416 Memoirs in *Methodist Magazine* 1818.

417 Letter to G. Shadford 1773.

418 Letter to Thomas Rankin 1 March 1775.

419 Letter sent via Rankin 1 March 1775.

420 *Some Observations on Liberty: occasioned by a late tract* 1776.

421 *A Seasonable Address to the Inhabitants of Great Britain by a Lover of Peace* 1776.

422 Account of his life edited in Stephens *Lives of the early Methodist Preachers* 1903.

423 Said to the Methodist preacher Martin Rodda after his arrest for being an outspoken Royalist.

424 JW *Journal* 1 Nov 1788.

425 Cited in T. Jackson *Life of Rev Charles Wesley* Vol II 1842.

426 Quoted in D.M.Jones *Charles Wesley* 1920.

427 Letter to Bishop of London 10 Aug 1780.

428 Quoted in A.C.H. Seymour *The Life and Times of Selina Countess of Huntingdon* 1839.

429 Letter to JWF and his wife 21 June 1784.

430 *Memoir of the Rev. Charles Atmore* Wesleyan Methodist Magazine 1845.

431 *On Separation from the Church* 30 Aug 1785.

432 Letter to Dr Chandler 28 April 1785.

433 Published posthumously. Lines were in possession of the preacher Samuel Bradburn.

434 Letter to JW 8 Sept 1785.

435 Sermon 114 and repeated in JW's biography of Fletcher.

436 Letter to Henry Moore 11 May 1788.

437 From manuscript verse (Hymn IX) in F. Baker: *Representative Verse of CW* 1962.

438 First published by the doctor who attended him and later set to music as the hymn 'Trust in Jesus'.

439 T. Jackson *The Life of the Rev Charles Wesley* 1841.

440 In the introduction to the 1816 edition of his sermons.

441 JW *Journal* 6 July 1789.

442 From the official account of his last days written by Elizabeth Ritchie.

443 Quoted in R.Watson *The Life of Rev. John Wesley* 1835.

444 Based on words in her journal.

445 From Prayer for Monday morning in *Prayers for Children* 1777.

446 From 'After Time Negligently and Unprofitably Spent' Nov 1752.

447 From Prayer for Tuesday morning in *Prayers for Children* 1777.

448 From Prayer for Sunday evening in *A collection of forms of prayer for every day in the week* 1733.

449 From Prayer for Monday morning in *A collection of forms of prayer for every day in the week* 1733.

450 This prayer is one of a number in *An Account of Mrs Elizabeth Johnson* 1799.

451 Based on her writings.

452 From Prayer for Thursday morning in *A collection of forms of prayer for every day in the week* 1733.

453 *Sermons collected in Discourses on Important Subjects* Vol II 1823

454 Based on hymn 'Weary of wandering from my God' in *Hymns and Sacred Poems* 1749.

455 From Prayer for Monday evening in *A collection of forms of prayer for every day in the week* 1733.

456 Phrases found in manuscript *Prayer for Truth* in John Ryland's Library, Manchester.

457 Written on his first journey to America to support the work of John Wesley in 1737.

458 From 'Lord that I may learn from thee' in *Short Hymns from select passages of Holy Scripture*' 1762.

459 Widely attributed to him.

460 From her *Journal* 16 Jan 1765.

461 From *An extract of letters* 1769.

462 From manuscript diary of Mary Entwisle 10 Sept 1797 John Ryland's Library, Manchester.

463 M.D.McMullen *Prayers and Meditations of Susanna Wesley* 2000.

464 Cited in S.Pellowe: *A Wesley Family Book of Days* 1994 Renard.

465 Translated in M. Counsell *2000 Years of Prayer* 1999 Canterbury Press.

466 *Wesley Banner* pg 766.

467 From Prayer for Thursday evening in *A collection of forms of prayer for every day in the week* 1733.

468 Widely attributed to him.

469 From his covenant prayer. Full text in F. Cook *William Grimshaw of Haworth* 1997.

470 From 'Forth in thy name, O Lord' in *Hymns and Sacred Poems* 1749.

471 Widely attributed to him.

472 Susanna Designe's *Journal* 18 Aug 1741.

473 Covenant Prayer 1755.

474 From 'Father, Son and Holy Ghost' in *Hymns on the Lord's Supper* 1745.

475 From prayer for Sunday morning in *Prayers for Children* 1777.

476 From prayer for Sunday evening in *Prayers for Children* 1777.

477 From 'See, Gracious Lord' in *Poetical Works of John and Charles Wesley* Vol II 1869.

478 Modernised verse from 'Saviour I joyfully agree' in *Poetical Works of J & C Wesley* Vol IX 1869.

479 Widely attributed to him.

480 From prayer for Thursday morning in *Prayers for Children*' 1777.

481 From prayer for Monday morning in *Prayers for Children* 1777.

482 From 'Come my soul with every care', a hymn written in 1779.

483 From a prayer by a preacher as remembered by her

1779.

484 From 'O Thou who camest from above' in *Short Hymns on select passages of Holy Scripture* 1762.

485 From M.D.McMullen *Prayers and Meditations of Susanna Wesley* 2000

486 From Prayer for Friday morning in *A collection of prayers for families* 1784.

487 Based on writings in her journal.

488 From prayer for Tuesday evening in *A collection of prayers for families* 1784.

489 From prayer for Thursday evening in *A collection of prayers for families* 1784.

490 From 'Christ from whom all blessings flow' in *Hymns and Sacred Poems* 1740.

491 Modernised verse from 'Jesus thy servants bless' in *Poetical Works of J & C Wesley* Vol XII 1869.

492 Modernised verse from 'Forth in thy strength, O Lord' in *Poetical Works of J & C Wesley* Vol I 1869.

493 From M.D. McMullen *Prayers and Meditations of Susanna Wesley* 2000

494 From 'Glory, love, and praise and honour' in *Poetical Works of J & C Wesley* Vol III 1869.

495 From 'Be present at our table, Lord' written c1741.

496 From a prayer for Wednesday evening in *Prayers for Children* 1777.

497 From 'God be mercifully near' in *Poetical Works of J & C Wesley* Vol VIII 1869.

498 From a prayer for Saturday evening in *Prayers for Children* 1777.

499 From Hymn CI in *Olney Hymns* 1779.

500 From prayer for Saturday evening in *A collection of prayers for every day of the week* 1733 (modernised version).

Index

This lists the people who are quoted (black) and/or illustrated (red)

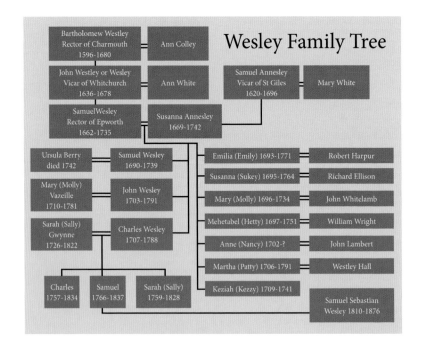